Memoirs

Memoirs

of
Grace Flandrau

Introduction by Georgia Ray

St. Paul, Minnesota • Knochaloe Beg Press • 2003

© 2003 by Georgia Ray dba Knochaloe Beg Press
315 Salem Church Road
St. Paul, Minnesota 55118
All rights reserved.
Manufactured in the United States of America
10 9 8 7 6 5 4 3 2 1
Library of Congress Control Number: 2003110325
(Hardcover) ISBN 0-9744258-0-X   (Paperback) ISBN 0-9744258-1-8

About Knochaloe Beg

Knochaloe Beg (*nuhKAYlow beg,* meaning "small, fragrant hill") is a farm on the Isle of Man, owned by the descendants of Philip Corrin for over 250 years. Grace Corrin Hodgson Flandrau visited the ancestral farm at least twice in her life. She described Knochaloe Beg in 1930s correspondence to relatives and in her prize-winning 1942 *New Yorker* short story, "What Do You See, Dear Enid?"

Flandrau's grandmother, Charlotte Corrin, and her two older sons, Edward John (Grace's father) and Thomas Corrin (Grace's uncle), were born at Knochaloe Beg during the first half of the nineteenth century.

On the cover

Grace Flandrau, from a photograph in the *St. Paul Daily News* (April 25, 1915) adapted from a portrait by C. H. Wiebmer.

Illustration credits

Endsheets (hardcover only): (left) view of Paris from the French school attended by Grace Flandrau as a child and (right) the "tall handsome doors" of the school, photos by Marie-Noël Laurent; (background) handwritten letter, Grace Hodgson to Drusilla (Drucy) Hodgson, December 18, 1900, courtesy of Corrin Haley Hodgson and Harold Lewis Nelson.

Frontispiece (p. ii) and p. 90: courtesy of the Arizona Historical Society Library, Tucson; p. 2: courtesy of the Minnesota Historical Society; p. 24: #933, Alfred Atmore Pope Collection, Hill-Stead Museum, Farmington, Connecticut; p. 122: photo by Robert L. Wolff.

Copy-editing, design, & production
Ellen Green, E. B. Green Editorial, St. Paul

Printing & binding
Sexton Printing, Muscle Bound Bindery, and Midwest Editions

Contents

Preface

Grace Flandrau's drafted but never-published memoirs turned up unexpectedly in the late 1980s during my research for her biography in the Flandrau Family Papers at the Arizona Historical Society in Tucson.[1] Two bulging file folders in the St. Paul author's personal papers contained dozens of loose, draft-typed onionskin pages of her recollections of youth. With Flandrau's handwritten changes in ink and pencil, the unnumbered, undated sheets were in various stages of completion. Apparently she worked on them for years and seldom threw away a draft.

Because it took so much time to sort through the faded, repetitious material and because reconstruction of Flandrau's personal and literary stories seemed more important, I did not immediately understand the quality of the prose I had stumbled upon or its strategic place in the author's career. After four research trips to Tucson, I had deciphered only enough of the loose autobiographical material to use as background and quotes for the biography.

Finally, in spring 1990, I began working through the two neglected folders, selecting more extensive chunks of Grace Flandrau's reminiscences for copying than I had before. As I proceeded with ordering and transcribing the raw material I had brought home to Minnesota, realization dawned and certainty grew that I had found a literary treasure.

The next year, while visiting the Firestone Library at Princeton University for research in the Charles Scribner's Sons Archive, I delved into the 1930s correspondence between Grace Flandrau and Maxwell E. Perkins, executive editor of Scribner's at that time. To my amazement I found letters between Flandrau and Perkins in late 1936 and early 1937 discussing the very autobiographical drafts I had found in the author's papers in Tucson.[2]

While Perkins's preference for a novel discouraged Grace from completing her memoirs, the distinguished prose of her drafts convinced me to seek a wide audience for the material.

The reminiscences are Flandrau's prose verbatim. My work has consisted of:

1. sorting through the material for the most complete and polished drafts while searching for thematic and chronological sequence
2. dividing the material into three main segments by subject
3. ordering each segment with interior chapter headings
4. in one or two cases, finishing a sentence where Flandrau indicated a choice of phrases or words or omitted a word
5. adding French accents (Flandrau was fluent in French and after World War II wrote scripts in French for the *Voice of America*, but she set aside her memoirs before attending to such details.)

6. light copy-editing (for spelling, punctuation, and occasional redundancy).

Waiting as long as I did to transcribe these poignant reminiscences allowed my reconstruction of Grace Flandrau's life and literary stories to help me place the work chronologically in her career path and understand what motivated her to draft but never finish them.

Along the road from puzzlement to clarity regarding Grace Flandrau's story, I received encouragement, enlightenment, and financial support from many. I am most grateful to Flandrau descendants in Tucson for granting me permission to publish this work.[3]

The Saint Paul Foundation provided a challenge grant in 1989. Other local foundations and several private donors met that challenge, and then a second in 1991: the Alice M. O'Brien Foundation, the Richard C. Lilly Foundation, the Mary Livingston Griggs and Mary Griggs Burke Foundation, the Northern Star Foundation, the Marbrook Foundation, the Benlei Foundation, Kate S. Klein, Kate K. Piper, Olivia I. Dodge, Judson and Barbara W. Bemis, Constance S. Otis, Margaret B. Brooks, Markell Brooks, John C. and Jeanette Burton, Lyman E. Wakefield Jr., W. B. and Patricia R. Saunders, Albert W. Lindeke Jr., and Grace Flandrau's cousins Corrin H. Hodgson, Muriel E. Nelson, the late Harold E. Nelson, and the late Ruth H. Cadwell all provided financial aid. Most contributed more than once.

The Minnesota Historical Society (MHS) made an early grant to support the work, and its archivists, editors, and librarians, as well as those at the Arizona Historical Society in Tucson, the Firestone Library at Princeton University in Princeton, New Jersey, the Beineke Rare Books Library at Yale University in New Haven, Connecticut,

Hamline University in St. Paul, and the Hill-Stead Museum in Farmington, Connecticut, have been unfailingly helpful. In addition to financial assistance, Grace Flandrau's relatives and Flandrau descendants in Arizona have contributed genealogical charts, photographs, and memories of vital importance to reconstructing the author's lost story.

Thanks to fellow Flandrau historian Lawrence Peter Haeg, whose insights and gift of a copy of his unpublished biography of Charles Flandrau have been immensely helpful, and to Persis Fitzpatrick for assistance with French accents.

I also gratefully acknowledge the help of computer technicians including my son, Don DeCoster III; my daughter Claire; my niece and her husband, John and Jane Ransom; my son-in-law Perry M. Beider; Deborah Griffith, our housekeeper; Karrie L. Galetka of Mouse Calls; and Josh Doughty of The Geek Squad.

Special thanks to the literary professionals who have become my friends and Grace Flandrau's: Gail See, a partner of Ruminator Press; Jane and Dick Noland of Partners Four; Jean A. Brookins, retired director of MHS Press; Ellen B. Green, my first editor and now book packager/copy-editor for these memoirs; John M. Roth, intellectual property attorney; and Anne R. Kaplan and Marilyn Ziebarth, editors of *Minnesota History* magazine.

Finally, I want to thank my husband, Albert W. Lindeke Jr., for listening to and commenting on biographical drafts and memoirs, for providing me with a wonderful office over our garage, and for believing that I would finish the work some day.

—Georgia Ray

Introduction

Grace Flandrau's never-published reminiscences of her youth are the only existing examples of her autobiographical, nonfiction prose. She drafted them during the years in which she produced her best published writing—autobiographical short fiction and creative nonfiction for magazines like *Scribner's,* the *New Yorker,* and *Harper's* (1930–1945). Except for short descriptive passages in speeches during those years, terse comments to reporters, and letters to one or two intimates in her old age, the author shared few glimpses of her private life, especially of her childhood. In fact, St. Paulites who knew her remember Grace Flandrau more for her chronic secrecy than for candor.[1]

The rare frankness and quality of Flandrau's memoirs, therefore, raise these questions:

1. Who was Grace Flandrau and what training did she have as a writer?
2. Why did she, at age thirteen, attend a convent school in Paris?

3. What or who motivated Flandrau to draft and redraft her memoirs, only to abandon the project before completion?
4. Why is the talented author of these memoirs largely forgotten?

More than a decade of research in the author's papers in six archives across the United States and extensive interviews with Flandrau family associates and their descendants demonstrate that, despite the praise she won elsewhere, Grace Flandrau never attained much credibility as a writer in her hometown, at least not with those who counted most—the St. Paul press and aristocratic literati. Instead, skepticism and disapproval clouded her local reputation, both as a writer and as a member-by-marriage of the city's high society.

Fueling that entrenched disregard was the antipathy of her brother-in-law, Charles Macomb Flandrau. The influential Charles, a celebrated early-twentieth-century American essayist and beloved columnist for St. Paul newspapers, mentored Grace at the start of her career before World War I. Initially, he was proud of her. As her fame grew, however, Charles became secretly jealous and disdainful of Grace's quest for popular success. His views about other rival Minnesota authors, Sinclair Lewis and Scott Fitzgerald, were similarly negative. Ironically, although both Grace and Charles Flandrau were gifted writers—erudite, witty masters of language—today they occupy almost equally dim status in Minnesota's literary memory.[2]

Fate provided stiff challenges as well as unusual advantages to the wide-eyed St. Paul native Grace Hodgson, born in her father's home at 518 Dayton Avenue in 1886. Her scholastic and performing talents were noteworthy in childhood. As a girl, Grace read to herself from morning to night. By the age of twelve she had devoured Dickens,

Shakespeare, and Browning—works she found in her father's library.[3]

Grace's father, Edward J. Hodgson—a lawyer and businessman as well as a scholar, born on the Isle of Man—was a strong influence on her academic and social development. He insisted on French and music lessons after school for his daughters and read aloud to them at night. A foster daughter, Lucile, niece of Hodgson's wife, lived with the family. She was two years older than Grace.

Edward's wife, Mary Staples Hodgson, whom he met at Hamline University in Red Wing, was not Grace's birth mother. Instead, Edward's mistress, Anna Redding Hodson, a young widow from one of the Dakotas (originally from Saratoga, New York), bore his daughter, but that was a closely guarded secret for many years.[4]

Edward Hodgson, who always thought of himself as an Englishman, enjoyed financial success and prominence as founder of a St. Paul law firm in the 1870s, a real estate development partnership in the 1880s, and the Security Trust Company, a mortgage bank, in 1891. He was also a prolific, much-published contributor to Minnesota newspapers and English literary magazines, and he dabbled in state politics.

Although Edward's stepfather, Thomas Hodgson, was an immigrant Dakota County farmer originally from the Isle of Man, Edward Hodgson's birth father was an English aristocrat, and his mother, Charlotte Corrin—a member of the Manx landed gentry—reputedly was a descendant of Viking kings. Edward's single-minded quest for upward mobility—financial and social—strongly imprinted Grace's childhood.[5]

When his bank failed in the Panic of 1893, Hodgson narrowly escaped bankruptcy. Suffering severe financial reverses, he sent his wife,

Mary, and her maiden sister Jennie, with Grace and Lucile, to live in Paris (1900–1903). Mary was to place the girls in school there; living cost less in Europe than in the United States. With his family away, Hodgson and the Security Trust Company gradually recovered solvency, and Anna Redding Hodson, who had given birth to Edward's son, William, in 1892, moved to Minneapolis with her boy. But Edward soon fell victim to cancer and died in fall 1903, just after his wife returned to St. Paul with Grace and Lucile.

Upon her father's death, Grace, age seventeen, may have learned for the first time that Edward's wife was not her birth mother. At any rate, she continued to live and travel extensively with her father's widow in the years before her marriage to Blair Flandrau. When Grace entered St. Paul's socially prominent Flandrau family as a bride in 1909, she introduced Mary Hodgson to her in-laws and their friends as her mother, not as her stepmother. Evidently Edward Hodgson's relatives had advised young Grace to take this course and thus erase Anna Redding Hodson from her life.[6]

Grace did connect with her birth brother, William Hodson, in 1932, twenty-three years after her marriage. By then William, a graduate of Harvard Law School, was a nationally known social worker in Manhattan. When Blair Flandrau learned from Grace about her illegitimacy and her birth brother, he was not in the least perturbed, though St. Paul society undoubtedly was.[7]

To most people nowadays there is little scandal in this human story. Love children have never been uncommon, even in royal households. What shocked St. Paul in the 1930s was that upon Edward Hodgson's death his double life emerged as just short of bigamous. This is one reason that the descendants of Flandrau friends who knew

Grace remember that she never talked about her father—an acute hardship since she had adored him.

After she became a famous American writer and gained the courage for honesty, Grace referred to her childhood as "anomalous," a fitting word for a family life that even today would be considered, if not scandalous, at least disturbingly unconventional. As a child she coped with gossiping neighbors who suspected her illegitimacy, her family's sudden extreme poverty, probable incest, and estrangement from her own relatives. Her story has the mistaken-identity quality of a Gilbert and Sullivan operetta with the dark overtones of the novels of Charles Dickens. The adult Grace, who could identify with almost any human problem, was famous for her empathy with young people and unfailingly earned their affection. No wonder she became a writer.[8]

To understand what motivated Flandrau in middle age to speak about her childhood, one must take a magnifying glass to the years just before and during which she drafted her memoirs—the early to mid-1930s. A close study of her literary career in that period reveals that she had the full attention and encouragement of the most prestigious publishing house in the United States—Charles Scribner's Sons of New York—through executive editor Maxwell E. Perkins and *Scribner's* magazine associate editors Kyle S. Crichton and Alfred S. Dashiell. Between 1927 and 1943 Grace Flandrau and these Scribner's editors exchanged over two hundred letters, more than eighty of them between Grace and Perkins.

Although Grace Flandrau's forte was short fiction, and *Scribner's* published a dozen of her short stories between 1930 and 1936, from 1930 on Maxwell Perkins tried to coax a full-length autobiographical novel from her. His persistence over the next seven years indicates he believed in her gifts as a writer.[9]

In mid-1935 Charles Scribner's Sons published Thomas Wolfe's *Of Time and the River*, a novel winning sincere praise from Flandrau. She lauded the book in a long letter to Perkins, admiring Wolfe's "truth and bigness of the point of view toward the characters. They are not judged, criticized, praised or blamed. They are accepted, and from that you get a breadth of feeling that is like life itself . . . I find it so satisfactory to be able to give all of my admiration at last to an American writer." Perkins replied with the confession that he had shown her letter to Tom Wolfe, who considered it the best of the fan letters he had received.[10]

In summer and fall 1936, and early 1937, Grace sought Perkins's advice about a new book. Her letters demonstrate clearly that she was basing her work on her own life story and that she was thinking of using "memoir" as her medium. Late in 1936 she wrote Perkins:

I want to ask your opinion and advice about a very important thing. I find that one whole section of my book, as yet only blocked out, could be conveniently taken out and put forward separately . . . It is almost wholly autobiographical. The point is, is it wiser to present it in the first person or in fiction form? As autobiography or as a novel?

There are several things, it seems to me, to be said on both sides. It deals with my girlhood in France, briefly, and the four years we were in Mexico during the beginning of the Mexican revolution . . . Do you think people like to read things written in the first person as well as if it is presented as fiction?

Now, if it is written as thinly disguised fiction, it gives me much more leeway. On the other hand, to write it as a straight reminiscence could give it a certain ease and simplicity. And value too . . .

Please write me what you think. I suppose Wolfe's books are almost pure autobiography, aren't they? Yet he has used the fiction form.

Anyhow, I shall be eager to have your opinion, especially as to the relative chances of getting it <u>read</u>. Which form . . . would be most apt to sell well? As a "memoir" it would be necessarily a little less personal, I mean as to the inner events . . . Do let me have your opinion.[11]

Perkins replied:

Although I do not fully understand the problem that confronts you—that is, I do not understand the relations between this narrative about a girl's life in France and the Mexican episode and the complete novel—I am pretty well convinced that the narrative should be in the form of fiction because of the different and deeper quality that that form seems to give. There is also the practical reason, which always intrudes itself upon a publisher, that unless a reminiscent volume has some other features that give it salience aside from that of quality, it is very hard to get attention for it, or a sale. But in fiction the question of the intrinsic quality counts for far more.

I shall think over the question some more, and maybe you will tell me more about it, but I am sure that put in the form of fiction it would be more effective and wiser, unless you have strong reasons on the other side that may develop.[12]

Alas, that was then, this is now. Because autobiographical fiction was what he hoped for from Grace, Perkins evidently never saw her memoir drafts. Although she quickly informed him that she would handle her story as fiction as he advised, Grace dropped the project entirely. Perhaps she decided her subject was too sensitive and abandoned the book for that reason.[13]

Understandably, Flandrau was reluctant to dispute Perkins's advice; once before she had done so, with discouraging results. Also, memoir in the 1930s was not the highly favored literary genre it has become in recent years. Grace was ahead of her time, ahead even of one of America's most brilliant editors. That accident is just one example of her star-crossed fate as a writer.[14]

Scribner's magazine ceased publication in 1936, and that year Maxwell Perkins recommended agent Carl S. Brandt of Brandt and Brandt, New York, to Grace. Her short autobiographical fiction and essays appeared soon and for the next eight years in such magazines as *Harper's,* the *New Yorker, Collier's, Good Housekeeping, McCall's, Yale Review, Holiday,* and *American Quarterly.* After 1945, declaring that she didn't like fiction and seldom read it, Flandrau turned her career toward journalism and public speaking. After receiving awards for her literary achievements in the late 1940s, Flandrau ceased writing for publication.[15]

The voluminous collection of unfinished, unpublished reminiscences, lying unread in Grace Flandrau's papers for more than half a century, testifies to her need to divulge the long-repressed story of her youth. The work also represents Flandrau at her highest level of attainment as a prose artist and for that reason demands exposure. The following vignettes and stories of the author's youth bring readers their first opportunity to hear this Minnesota artist's provocative voice at its most authentic.

Memoirs of Grace Flandrau

Edward J. Hodgson, Grace's father

Child Memories

1. Childhood

In our family I was the pet, the spoiled darling, the royal favorite. My father was the Victorian patriarch, the tyrant, the ruler by divine right, and I was subject to no discipline except the sudden, unreasonable lightnings of his uncertain temper.

You see a thin, small, high-strung, emotional child, with big shining eyes, a broad forehead, surly, self-indulgent lips, a pointed chin. Intensely loving, hot-tempered, too full of laughter, and too easily hurt. I sing, I recite, I play the violin, I speak pieces.

The house is full of company. I am lifted high above their heads and made to stand on top of a big iron safe, an empty safe, one kept for no known reason in the corner of the living room. Perched up there above them all I recite long poems, dramatically, with gestures, to which relatives and guests are compelled to listen. I have a fabulous memory for verse. It seems natural for me to be up there above everybody else, speaking pieces with all the faces lifted to me. There is only one person to whom I am not superior, and this is my father. I am the royal mascot.

I always have a best friend, a little girl with whom I play continuously when she is available, but if there is no child, I am not discontented but spend long hours in the tops of the apple trees and maple trees, swarming through the branches of the trees in the yard and smelling the roses. Climbing up, up especially, if I can, oak trees, which is my only outdoor passion. Climbing up, up, never satisfied if there is a branch above me that will hold my weight. Eventually one doesn't, and I fall, perhaps thirty feet, but nothing, happily, is broken by the impact.

Indoors I read, I read from morning 'til night, uninterruptedly, and at night he reads aloud to me. It is understood the others may listen if they care to, but the reading is for me alone. I sit on his lap with my arm around his neck, my head on his breast, divinely happy and secure.

He drives up one day in a handsome hired carriage, with prancing horses and silver chains. I am invited to drive with him into the country. No one else is invited. This seems natural and to be expected as my mother and sister are to stay at home.

My violin teacher sends word that there is grand opera in Chicago, that she is going, and it would be good for us to go along. I am sent, but not my sister, though she is the natural musician. But that is as it should be, part of the tradition, going back to earliest childhood.

This then must be one of the threads—this favoritism, this suppression of the rights of others, the subordination of the pleasure of others to me alone must be one inexorable part of the pattern. Perhaps you shudder already for the man who is going to marry the spoiled darling, and I do not blame you. But there were many other threads, and the pattern took many different shapes.

There was the vague and never-quite-faced question of poverty. It was a tradition in the household that although there was generally not enough money for the barest necessities, there was always enough for the luxuries. When we had not food enough to eat or money to pay for warm clothes and coal to heat the house, we had nevertheless a French governess. When my father was staving off the bank, we gave a large dinner for the governor of the state. When we had visitors from England, my father drove them about in a hired brougham, and my mother ran up incredible bills for fine linen at the best department stores.

We were poor. My father drove himself as no galley slave has ever done to stave off bankruptcy, to which he would under no circumstances resort. But "I'm ruined," he would cry, driving the blood from my heart. "The game is up. We'll all starve to death. We're going to the poor house."

But at other times he talked suavely and like a rich man, how he would buy fine horses and especially statues. He preferred, he said, statuary to painting. He would build a mansion on the bluff, with stained-glass windows and a porte cochere. That we should be about to starve and also about to buy mansions and statuary seemed as plausible as anything.

And at the time when we were poorer than any other, when my father came home at nine or ten o'clock at night, white, exhausted, with a look of anguish on his beautiful thin face, suddenly it was announced that he was sending all three of us to Europe to Paris to school. A perfect French accent was the indispensable attribute of gentility.

2. Travel in France and the Orient

A phrase that was particularly favored in our family was "travel is so educational." Like most much-quoted phrases it is, I think, quite false. I don't mean to say travel cannot be educational, to use that vaguely offensive word; I merely say that as travel is generally indulged in, it certainly is not. It certainly was not in our family. If it had been educational, I, at the age of twenty, should have been a candidate for the Academy of Arts and Sciences.

Our world travel began when I was twelve. It began when my gentle, innocent, timid, adventurous mother, my somewhat acid but nevertheless valuable spinster aunt, my older sister, and I embarked for several years of travel and education in the Old World. The education was to be obtained in schools in Paris.

To this end I was deposited—eventually, my sister always managed to wiggle out of things like that—in an ancient school that without doubt was the worst school extant at the time. The one or two others at which I was previously checked were the second and third worst schools in the universe. These schools were fantastic places in their different lethal ways, and how children survived them physically or morally is rather a mystery.

But all that is another question and has no place in this reminiscence. Suffice it to say that the only thing well-taught in any of these schools was the French language. There were some vague references to history—the history, of course, of France. We learned that French kings, generals, statesmen, scholars, and artists were the only kings, generals, statesmen, scholars, and artists of importance the world had ever seen—with the exception of any who might have had revolutionary tendencies. These, including one insignificant and rascally fellow named Voltaire, were beneath any notice beyond a few words of blasting condemnation. As to the others, we learned nothing in particular about them except that they existed and were superior to all others of their kind in whatever land.

There were no bathtubs in this school (the last one, in which I spent two years), no central heating, no lights except candles above the ground floor. The school building had thick walls and sagging floors, and its deeply recessed iron-barred windows looked out onto narrow gothic streets in one of the city's oldest quarters. The staircase by which I climbed to my cell was built in the twelfth century and the rest of the building a few hundred years later, and not a window had been opened since it was completed.

Between school terms in Europe, there was travel. We were taken to Italy, to Switzerland, to the British Isles, to various parts of France, but I was always redeposited at school in Paris at the beginning of the term to resume my studies.

But however that may be, and in spite of the starvation rations— eels in brown sauce every other Friday was the high spot—those years have left stamped on my heart a love for France and the French people and the French way of life that exceeds all other loves. When I am among French people in France—French people in other countries are no longer the same, they undergo some sea change that is generally for the worse—they seem to be more my own than any others. Their ways, if not always perfect or even admirable, are to me supremely comprehensible, as American ways so often are not.

When we left France and returned to America nearly five years had passed. I was sixteen and a stranger in my own country, filled with nostalgic dismay at ways I did not wholly understand. And I returned to see my father die.

And then we were on the wing again. For my mother, as for so many other American widows, travel had become an avocation, an excuse, and a change. We went back and forth across the continent, to California and on across the Pacific. The few intervening years before my marriage were spent chiefly on trains and boats.

All this went on although the family conviction was at all times that we were desperately poor. That any of us might strike out and earn a living had simply never been considered. It had been completely outside my father's exalted ideas of gentility. That his girls should ever have to work had been so unthinkable to him that he had never allowed it to emerge into consciousness.

When we got back from Europe I begged my mother to send me to boarding school, but she declared we were so desperately poor she could not afford it. "No, I really don't know how we'll manage," mother said, scaring me dreadfully.

But the year she refused to send me to boarding school she bought me a thousand-dollar Amati violin. That year we were also engaged in interminable journeyings about the United States, making visits upon rather surprised friends, distant relatives, and even slight acquaintances.

The following year we set sail across the Pacific to Hawaii, to Japan and China, and to the Philippine Islands. We traveled in a private sitting room on the boat. In Japan we traveled with a private courier, who waited upon us like queens and served us exquisitely dainty meals in our private compartment in first-class railway carriages.

There was a pleasant tour into Korea, there were weeks of horse-back riding, dancing in Shanghai, and there was much entertaining in

Hong Kong where the British regiment, the "Buffs," was stationed. Members of the regiment to whom we were introduced took us to races, polo matches, and gymkhanas.

There was the carnival in Manila and fancy dress balls at the fort—I forget what its name was. A whole winter was spent in a house in Bubbling Well Road in Manila, a winter of such ease and gaiety as I had not yet known, with number-one and -two and -three and -four houseboys, all costing less than one hired girl in Minnesota.

We attended balls and dinners and paper chases on Saturday afternoons across a countryside that was misted in a sad brown rain. We had endless clothes made by Chinese tailors because they were so good and so cheap, and we came back to America loaded with Japanese kimonos, Chinese lion skins, Korean rosewood chests, carved ivory, teakwood, and bronze jars.

Soon after we returned to St. Paul, mother was heard moaning, "I don't know what's going to happen to us. I think we ought to go to stay with Grandma for a year. I really don't know how we'll manage otherwise."

At Grandma's I had to fight off a trip to Alaska, which mother suddenly decided she would like to take. Instead, I returned to St. Paul and got engaged.

3. Engagement

I was nineteen, and I had been in and out of love several times. Of what is called learning I knew nothing except the French language. I spoke French like a French girl, with a perfect accent and complete fluency. I knew something of the great books Father had read aloud when I was a child, and I did like to read—in a desultory way I had read a good deal. I could play the violin fairly well for an amateur.

In no school, however, had I learned anything. Neither in school nor out had I received any discipline. I was idle, and I was spoiled. I was used to being amused and to being waited upon. I could not sew, and I could not even pack. I had seen something of the world but as one might witness a pageant being played upon a stage. It related to nothing.

My state would scarcely be worth dwelling upon if it had not been so much more usual for young girls to be as I was then than it is now. I was a product of the times. All his life my father had been haunted by one hideous fear—that I might have to go out into the world and make my own living. I was not haunted by this fear because I could not conceive of destiny daring to play me such a trick.

And now I was back in Minnesota. When I walked along the quiet, shady, so-American streets at twilight, hearing the growl of the lawn mower, smelling the new-cut grass wet with the dazzling spray of the industriously turning sprinkler, the spectacle would fill me with a kind of detached—and also amused—horror. A duplex, a husband in shirtsleeves mowing the lawn while the baby staggers about in rompers, and in the kitchen mother fries the beefsteak, the smell of which floats out and mixes with the evening odors of wet grass and dusty streets and summer foliage—it was a picture of a life to which I could no more be condemned than to that of a coolie woman, balancing her pails of night soil, still slumbering, as she pads out to fertilize her few square yards of garden.

But although I knew so well what I did not want, I had formed no idea at all of what I did want. Nor had I been, indeed, conscious of wanting any special thing I did not have until that sunny afternoon when I sat under an apple tree among twinkling poplars, reading a book called *Viva Mexico!* Even then it was not so much a wish as a certainty that this very thing should be mine.

Someone had put this book in my hand when I left the house where I was visiting that morning. *Viva Mexico!* was not a long book, and I knew that the author [Charles M. Flandrau] lived in St. Paul and that I had met him a few times when I had been there before. But he had seemed to me, frankly, to be a middle-aged person, and his brother, Blair, whom I had seen only once, had also seemed somewhat removed in age from myself.

I do not think I appreciated at that time the wit or the high sophistication of the book's style. I only realized that I was transported into a world as completely different from the duplex-on-Kent world of lawn mowers that aroused my special derision as it was possible to reach, as different in its way as China, and with the added poignance or beauty of seeing it not, so to speak, in the flesh but given form as filtered through the eyes of an authentic and rare artist.

And when I came to the chapter that is a letter from a coffee plantation deep in the semitropical jungle of Mexico, the odd certainty suddenly took possession of me that I should go there soon and that it would be my home, accessible only by mule travel across an intervening mountain, an endless trip. And, of course, I did and it was.

That my marriage [to William Blair Flandrau] should take me to a far-off land seemed, under the circumstances, nothing more than was to be expected, quite natural. Just to have married and settled down in St. Paul, Minnesota, was so outside of my habit that it just couldn't have come to pass. The sign of Mercury had always been and still is upon me.

Amusingly too, this curse of travel lasted almost until the moment of my marriage. I had invited a friend to make a trip with me on the Great Lakes just before I became engaged. And would she let me off? She would not. I cannot, until this day, endure the sight of a Great Lakes steamboat.

The marriage had to take place soon, before the coffee was ripe. But there had to be time for the inevitable trousseau. Mother came on from Grandmother's, protesting every mile of the way against this hasty and inexplicable purpose of getting married so suddenly and rushing off to a coffee plantation in Mexico to live. I was too young to marry anybody, she thought, and probably nobody knew better than she did that I was horribly spoiled and interested in nothing but gaiety and having a good time. A coffee plantation in the heart of the Mexican jungle—two days' mule ride from the nearest railway—was the last place on earth I should dream of going to.

At the same time I have no doubt Mother was already planning then that her next journey would take her to Mexico, as soon as it might be seemly.

I suppose Blair's family was equally dubious. What would I make of the life that had to be lived there?

But as all concerned were warm and indulgent people, nothing more serious than a few mild protests were made, and the wedding took place as soon as the trousseau could be made and the conventional amount of linen and silver secured and initialed in the time-honored way. Why linen and silver, under the circumstances, I don't know, except that it was the thing to do and therefore must be done.

What was this adventurous bride of nineteen years really like? We have spoken of my education, or lack of it, my reading and my travels, but, beyond being spoiled and untrained, what was my personality—my disposition—like?

I was in every essential without what is now called character training. I was, it is true, companionable. I liked to laugh, and I laughed a great deal and talked even more. I was vivacious and fairly amiable. I lost my temper quickly and as quickly got over it. Then as now I never kept a grudge. I think that may be a confession of weakness. There are grudges I ought to have kept and could not.

---

4. Visit to My Father's Grave

It is certainly significant that the day after I became engaged I went to the country to visit my father's grave. And the feeling that took me there was a subtle, exciting, secret thing. The visit had a romantic overtone, the quality, indeed, of a romantic tryst.

I had been, ever since I could remember anything, the little queen of the family, subject only to the capricious discipline of my father's temper. He was my father, mine. Nobody else's. There was a curious and profound sense of proprietorship. He belonged to nobody in the family except to me.

I have noticed this same attitude many times since. I have in mind a friend who was possessively devoted to his mother. And although intellectually he *knew*, of course, that she was the mother of his brothers, he did not *feel* it. She was his alone. And so, my father had been mine. He had existed only in relation to me.

The way [local] train had taken perhaps two hours to make the thirty-five mile trip to the small town where the cemetery was located. It stopped for long intervals at no place at all, just on the prairie, and, in the lovely quiet that followed, all the whirl of the hot wind and cinders blowing in the open windows, there was only the hum of the telegraph wires or the call of a bird, and back of the taint of soft coal smoke, you could smell the pure air, sweet with clover and wild roses and ripening grain.

The town I got off at wasn't really a town at all but only a general store, a blacksmith shop, a livery stable, and a water tank. Its station was so insignificant that to reach it from St. Paul there was nothing but one early morning train, and to leave there was only an evening train twelve hours later.

There were at that time no roads for motoring, so the country remained, even at short distances from the city, rustic and remote. To step off the train into the sudden large stillness of a tiny country station was to have traveled from one state of being into another—something that even the longest journey does not always procure for us now.

The stationmaster stared at me in surprise. I was not dressed for the country—something of which I had had in my life very little indeed. I was wearing a severely tailored suit made in Shanghai by one of those Chinese tailors who then copied clothes of all kinds for sums so fantastically small that touring mothers and daughters could only wonder why they hadn't had to die to reach this sartorial heaven.

The stationmaster looked at me, and I looked at him. His long, kindly, mule-shaped face, his eyes that were mere pinpoints of curiosity, his huge, strong, crooked teeth, the weathered, sunburnt flesh set in permanent wrinkles of cracker-barrel humor, and his air of deep vitality were so essentially Yankee and rural—the Yankee rustic of that time—that you could see him in any country town where you found Americans.

As I told him about the cemetery and the grave I had come to visit, lines of such intensely interested knowledge of me and my affairs spread over his features that it was like seeing a face photographed on film come into focus in developing fluid. He himself spoke my name and declared he would not only hitch up his team and drive me to the cemetery, but he would also come back for me at noon and take me to his "Paw's" for dinner.

Fine and fleet were the two black horses of his team, with flowing manes and tails that swept the ground. They wore fly nets of bright yellow and blue piping, gay with tassels and even having little caps fitted over the ears. Shuddering, the horses drove down their haunches with the merest touch of the whip, when the stationmaster flicked off a fly that was nipping between the yellow cords of the netting.

The road went straight as a ruler along the section line. The weeds and wildflowers, white with dust, shook with the wind of our passing, a wind that was as light as the dust that rose in delicate clouds behind us, stirred up by the flying hooves.

The summer day had the fullness of beauty that comes, it seems, only to northern lands. The sunlight was hot in the thin air, but a cool breeze stirred the silvery green ribbons of the rows of corn and spread like a wave over the tall meadow grass and the rosy blond wheat fields.

At the cemetery the stationmaster put me down and wheeled around his team with a great show of tossing heads and prancing fore-

feet. Then they flowed away back along the road as smoothly and rapidly as if they streamed before the wind.

I was alone. It is often a wonder to me that in a farm countryside,
where so much is growing and so much work is going on, there is so
little human movement to be seen. Here and there a great barn
bloomed rose-red through a faintly blue mist hovering over the fields.
A few cows, small as toys, stood knee-deep in a distant pond, and a
meadowlark insistently repeated its liquid phrase from the branches of
the tall poplar trees, but no creature moved and no human being was
to be seen within all the vast circle of the horizon.

The cemetery lay on a low, lopsided rise above the road. Two sides
were fenced with once-white pickets and a broken gate. A third side
was walled by a tall stand of corn, and the fourth merged into a sloping stretch of shining grass and wild flowers. If cemeteries must be, I
thought, they should all have the quiet peace of this one.

The burying ground itself was not well tended. It was like a garden
beside a neglected house where the owners have grown too old and
poor to prune and rake and restrain the weeds. Prairie flowers and the
descendants of once-planted garden flowers looked up from the
ragged wild vines and thistles. With incredible precision a striped go-
pher cocked himself up on a sagging headstone and, after an instant of
intense and palpitating watchfulness, whisked into the tangle of weeds
and disappeared.

The tomb I sought was more solid and newer than the others. It
had only been there a few years. I stood beside it, wondering at the
knowledge and pity and love I was at the moment possessed of.

People don't always hold on to their immediate love for their beloved dead. Much of the time it exists in the rich, deep treasure house

of the emotions into which one's conscious mind cannot enter at will, perhaps can never enter, but from which, from time to time, comes a love or sorrow or rage or joy to bring life and flowers, like Ceres's returning daughter, back to the arid, reasoned surface of the everyday.

Although I had been so young, or perhaps because I had been so young, I remembered everything my father had ever told me of his life. He had died four or five years earlier, when I was not quite fifteen. I had been separated from him for several years before that, so that most of my knowledge of him had been gained while I was a little girl. And to that, fifty years of living could have added little.*

I sat down beside the grave and leaned with my back against the stone. If there is one mystery in life, it is the mystery of love. Because love is wisdom, it is knowledge, it is the source of beauty. Indeed, love, in the impersonal sense, is life.

It is the curve of the line, the sound, the color, the form that distinguishes a work of art from just a painting, a statue or a symphony or, if you like, a business deal. It is the informing form that brings to life all products of the human spirit, whatever they may be. These works can be put together by some rule or rules learned out of a textbook, but they cannot be brought to life without this deep flow of the spirit, this illumined yes spoken to existence that can better be called love.

I had not known that I would meet the stationmaster/livery stable owner who would invite me for noon dinner at Paw's, so I had brought sandwiches and a book. Nor did I know that from that book would suddenly emerge a fantastic certainty as to the course of my future.

---

* Flandrau drafted these reminiscences in the late 1930s and early 1940s, when she was in her fifties.

Perhaps that is why genius remains forever close to childhood. Because for ordinary mortals it is only in childhood that this faculty or state of being or function of the spirit is available.

I had always loved my father with an excessive, almost violent, intensity. As I sat there, with my back against his tombstone, my awareness of the pity and love I felt for him filled me with an acute premonition of sorrow usually known only in dreams. I felt not only the confusion, the loss, the failure of my father's life but also the significance of it and how it was part of a time not quite passed, from which I myself had suffered and by which I felt myself throttled, stifled, and by which would suffer more in many simple and intricate ways.

All this I knew sitting there, and I found too what I have found since, that only in a graveyard does one experience deeply and without reason the hope of and belief in the immortal spirit. The sense of what lies there and what does not lie there offers a contrast that seems in itself a proof.

5. Dinner at Paw's

The sun had climbed high on the blue vault of the sky, its rays hotter and, by contrast, the breeze cooler. It was noon, and the air was more heavily sweet with all the summer smells.

Just as he had promised, the stationmaster was returning to fetch me for lunch at Paw's. Levelly along the straight road swept the two black horses, their yellow nets and their long tails flowing out behind them as they ran. The stationmaster loomed large on the high seat of the light, single-seated buggy.

Paw's house, alongside the rose-red barn and handsome outbuildings, had the stepchild look of most of the dwellings in this vicinity. A rough dirt road led into the yard. Under the shade trees the grass would not grow, and hundreds of stout, self-centered chickens strutted and picked, clucked and crowed, and made swift, unromantic love, with no softening of their hot, angry eyes. Dogs straight out of *McGuffey's First Reader*—a Newfoundland, a water spaniel, and a half-breed German shepherd—ran out to greet us, jumping and barking.

Over by the barns and the artesian well in the center of the yard it was neat, but around the house there was a rubbishy, untidy look. Some scraggly bachelor's buttons had been planted between the spokes of a discarded wheel. Bits of broken china and rusted machinery were strewn among the weeds that grew from the hard ground. Except for a man who was slowly leading a workhorse to the artesian well, the place looked deserted. But as we approached the house, we found it was humming with life. A screen door burst open, and out and down in one wild stride came a little girl in a wisp of calico, holding a younger child. Then, seeing us so near, she shrank against the wall. A fat infant sat in a baby carriage, pounding the edge with a spoon.

At the doorway, welcoming us, stood a stout, friendly woman. Behind her three or four young women flew about the kitchen while a vigorous-looking youth with a blue shirt open at the throat worked a small hand-pump at the sink. And already seated at the long table in the dining room was an old man. The stationmaster shouted to his father jovially, explaining who I was and why I was there. He had not bothered to do so with the women, an omission that was part of the man-to-man superiority of the time.

I don't know how many people sat down to the long dinner table—children, grandchildren, great-grandchildren, a girl from a neighboring farm who helped with the work, and three or four hired men. And all these people seemed as strange and remote from me as people from another planet. Farmers—a distinct class then and easily recognized. They did not go often to the city; they did not buy copies of copies of copies of Chanel models at the chain store in the village. There were no chain stores. There were few moving pictures, few automobiles. They looked and dressed and were different from city people, with a richer flesh, a greater tranquility, a look of rugged and yet explosive bodily strength.

The old man asked the blessing. His voice, instantly changed, took on a kind of evangelical meaning. All present bowed their heads and closed their eyes. Only the old man's daughter did not close her eyes; she sent a searching glance along the table, noting the plates piled high with thick slices of new bread, the dishes of crinkly blue glass with blue glass domes covering the butter, the green-tomato pickles, the cucumber and watermelon pickles, mounds of conserve and clear, salmon-colored jelly made from the crabapple trees in the yard. Laden plates were passed from hand to hand, starting with me.

The old man was deaf. "If you want more potatoes, Paw, just holler," yelled his son.

"Eh, what's that?"

"Potatoes. You holler. If you want more, holler."

And then, the stationmaster, forgetting to lower his voice or perhaps wishing to include the old man, turned to me. "Paw knew your grammaw and your paw too when he was a lad. Always said he'd never make a farmer, more like an actor fella with them fine features and that black hair and them blue eyes like his maw's." Shouting now, turning toward the old man, the stationmaster repeated. "Grammaw. She was quite a singer, you always said."

"It binds good, but it don't cut good," was the patriarch's singular reply.

But mostly the meal progressed in silence. The young women rose silently from time to time to bring in another steaming dish or replenish a platter. The young men never raised their eyes or spoke. The children stared shyly.

I could not eat. The stewed meat was tough, the fried ham too salty. The milk was too warm and had a strong taste, and the potatoes, having been fried in ham fat or maybe lard, had a flavor I was not accustomed to. It was incredibly hot. The butter melted, and the milk pitchers sweated. There were smells of frying pans and perspiration, of boiling coffee and children, and the sour smell of the baby. I felt faintly sick.

A stiff parlor with shut windows and a spare bedroom with a high-humped bed covered with a dazzling patchwork spread opened off the dining room. When the stationmaster's wife, with a kind smile that showed her teeth white against her moist, bright-red face, asked me if I would not like to rest there during the afternoon, I declined with haste.

I liked elegance at that time—delicate living, soft voices, perfume, and fine clothes. I wanted life to be as different as one could conceive from such humble and vital and physically earthy scenes as I had just taken part in. I wanted no part of work or of simple, humdrum family life and living.

I came the other day upon the poet's ironic phrase: "God is good. He gives us what we wanted yesterday." But perhaps He is as often cruel, when He gives us what we want today.

I was about to have my fondest wish come true—to live a romantic and glamorous life. But it was not destined to be a placid or easy or always enjoyable life.

Grace's French schooling influenced her sense of style for life.

Memories of a French School

1. Arrival

It was late afternoon when we got off the bus. An icy rain was turning to sleet, and the black wet sidewalk reflected the street lamps and the lights from the blurred shop windows. People were hurrying, with the water streaming from their raincoats and the bobbing roofs of their black umbrellas. They fought for places on the buses and tramways; conductors yelled the numbers, and the horses, straining to start the loaded vehicles, struck fire from the slippery cobblestones. There was even the music of some street fiddlers playing on the terrace of the big café.

But this was one of the oldest quarters of Paris, and right across the square it was dark and still. The gray face of the ancient church, the broken monuments, and dripping trees in the churchyard were dim behind the veil of rain.

"Don't look and don't dawdle," said the lady who was taking me to the school. "Here you are without rubbers, and we didn't even bring an umbrella."

She was a tall woman, and I had trouble keeping up with her as we hurried along the bright side of the square, I with one of my small suitcases, she with the other. At the corner we turned into a small dark street. It was so narrow you had to watch out for the big vans and buses that thundered past and made the ground shake under your feet. Uniform gray stone houses were flush with the sidewalk, and there were one or two tiny shops before whose windows the shining arrows of the rain would become suddenly visible.

Soon the lady stopped. "This is the number," she said, "but it certainly doesn't look like a school." It looked like all the other old houses except that a number of them seemed to have been joined together with only one entrance. Before us was a tall, handsome door, carved and trimmed with ornaments of iron. There was a big iron knocker, too high for me to reach, but I saw the wire with a wooden handle that hung down beside it. When I pulled on the wooden handle, I could hear the clamor of bells inside.

The door swung open of its own accord, and we went into a small bright antechamber. Then the door closed behind us. Away from the crash and rattle of the street it seemed startlingly quiet with only the faint whistling of the gaslight that hung from the ceiling and the rustle of papers where a young woman sat working at a desk. She wore a black dress buttoned up to the chin, knitted black wristlets, and a small black knitted cape about her shoulders. Her face was quite red as if it had been sunburned or come too near a fire.

"Inside, if you please," she said without looking up, nodding toward a pair of swinging doors.

It was a long, dim, low-ceilinged room we entered now, filled with greenish gaslight and the French row of heavily barred windows all along one wall. Dimly we could hear the roar and feel the rumble of the passing vehicles outdoors. Behind another desk at the far end of the room sat another woman, an old woman, or so it seemed to me, thin and upright, her smooth gray-black hair parted neatly down the middle, and her cheeks red with the same high color so often seen in French faces. My mother always declared it came from the red wine they drank.

"I am the new pupil," I said.

"Ah ha, the little American. Well, well. But you already speak like a French girl." She stared at me, half closing her eyes in a way near-sighted people have.

"Everything has been arranged," I told her.

"Yes, yes, I understood. Very well. I shall send then for someone to take you to your room."

"What does she say now?" inquired my escort.

"She says I'll be sent to my room," I answered.

"I don't suppose it will be necessary for me to go too," she wondered out loud. I asked the directress, and she shook her head.

"It would not be allowed. Tell Madame. No one goes inside but the pupils."

I explained, and the lady was relieved. "I'm late already, and it's such a horrible day. So I think—or perhaps I'd better wait 'til someone comes for you."

It was cold in the room and airless as if the air had been breathed over and over for I don't know how long. It had a smell too, that was, I would find, the smell of the school. Hard to describe but a little like the smell of old people mixed with the scent of food and coal gas.

"Ah, here is Mademoiselle Pitou," the woman at the desk murmured as another, younger, woman came into the room. They were, I noticed, dressed in identical costume. It was a black cloth dress with a full-gathered skirt and a bodice buttoned up the front to the top of the high collar over which was a small turnover of white trim. They too wore the knitted black wristlets under the long sleeves and small, black, knitted capes around their shoulders.

The school, I learned later, was run by a teaching order under the special patronage and protection of a cardinal in Rome. After the French government abolished religious schools in France—or tried to—a number of these women, who in reality were nuns, discarded the conventional costume. In some cases it was discarded so that the appearance of a lay school was given.

But aside from their dress, no two women could have been more dissimilar. Mademoiselle Pitou was a little, tightly corseted pudding of a woman with a plump, childish face. She watched me closely as my escort prepared to leave.

"Good-bye, Grace," the lady said. "Now, don't cry. Your mother is in Italy, and your father is in the United States, you know that. You are lucky to be attending a French school. Not many of the girls you know are privileged to attend a French school."

"So do you know when . . . ?"

"No. Try and appreciate your blessings, and don't bother your parents. Your father has lost a great deal of money, so don't expect much from anybody." She bent forward and kissed my cheek. The tip of her sharp nose was cold and a little wet.

"Good-bye."

Nodding vigorously to Mademoiselle Pitou and the lady at the desk, she again said good-bye in the loud voice she seemed to think would make English understandable to anybody. Then she hurried down the long room, embarrassed, I thought, by the noise her heels made on the bare floor, and went out without looking back.

Mademoiselle Pitou's needle eyes had not ceased to stare at me with intense curiosity. The kind of little eyes, I have noticed since, that see everything except the important things. "Well, come along then, my little miss. This way." Her voice was like the squeaking of an ungreased hinge, and she had a way of spitting her words from the end of her tongue, trilling her r's as they do in some of the provinces but not in Paris.

I started to pick up my bags.

"No, no—what an idea! The porter will take them." She raised her eyebrows toward Mademoiselle Lemay at the desk. "Naturally."

I was much embarrassed. And I wondered uneasily if I would be expected to give something to the porter. I had been left no money.

Mademoiselle Lemay said smoothly, "She means to be a good girl."

"Well, that we shall have to see. We shall have to wait and see."

In some curious way I felt superior to Mademoiselle Pitou. I knew, too, as infallibly as children do know, that we would never be either friendly or unfriendly and that, stupid as she was, she was not unkind.

We crossed the room to the door through which she had come. When she opened it and we went out, we stepped into another world, into something so profoundly and anciently French that the years I spent there, separated not only from my family but from all other Americans, were to make me always, to a slight degree, a stranger in my own country.

29

We went out first into the blowing, rainy darkness of an arcade, open along one side. Here and there a glass lantern equipped with gas was fastened to the dripping walls. In their dim light I could see that the gallery or cloister ran around the four sides of a square courtyard. And as we walked along this gallery what I noticed most was the soft, worn unevenness of the tiles under my feet. Indeed, this sensation is close to every memory of the school, for wherever it might be, whether it was tile or stone or the dark polished hard wood of the parquet floors, there was always this waviness, this silky softness made by the passing feet of many generations.

Midway along the gallery we came to a place where two buildings seemed to have been joined, and between them was an imposing staircase with stone treads and a wrought-iron rail that went up in majestic spirals. The lower steps were wet with the rain that blew in from the courtyard. All winter, I was to learn, an icy whirlwind whistled down the stairwell.

Mademoiselle Pitou paused with her yellow, pudgy, not-very-clean hand on the newel. "From the twelfth century, they say, this staircase," she said proudly and added, "but of course little Americans don't know anything about the twelfth century."

"But I do," I answered.

"You do?" She laughed. Her little pinpoint gaze so plunged into me it was as if she could not pull it out. "But how does that happen? And who knows if it is true?"

"It was a century marked in France by the rise, especially under Phillippe Auguste, of the royal ascendancy over the feudal lords. At this time, too . . ."

Mademoiselle Pitou began to laugh so hard that the pudding flesh above the steel walls of her formidable corset shook alarmingly. "Listen to her!" she cried. "Listen to this little one. And at this time what?"

I thought it silly of her to laugh like that. She had asked me what I knew and I had begun to tell her. I had spent all the preceding year in a walled garden back of the Invalides in the charge of a gentle young governess, a Frenchwoman whose passion was the history of France. And in the French fashion, I had learned my textbooks by heart.

" . . . and of the fall or expulsion from France of the Plantagenets. It was the beginning of the end too of English suzerainty in France. At this time the Plantagenets of England, of whom Richard the Lion-Hearted has had, perhaps, an undue share of fame . . . "

"Miséricorde!" cried Mademoiselle Pitou, still laughing. "Enough or I will have to make you a member of the French Academy, for the love of God."

Still cackling she began, wheezing and puffing, to climb the stairs. At the first broad turn a small door was set in the face of the stone wall. Pausing, she turned to ask me in a gasping whisper if I knew what it was and answered the question herself.

"It's the door to Mademoiselle de Vaugirard's apartment. And in case you don't know who she is, I will tell you that Mademoiselle de Vaugirard is head of everything, of this institution, and of them all."

"All what?"

"All the others. And what's more, you will be presented to her one of these days. And let me tell you, my young lady from America with all your Plantagenets, you will have to mind your manners when you're received by Mademoiselle de Vaugirard."

At the end of the second flight we turned down an open gallery and came to my room.

There were in this school two entirely separate departments. One was the school proper reserved for French girls. They slept in well-supervised dormitories and ate, studied, and played entirely apart from us, the foreign girls, the *étrangères,* as they called us. The French students did not, indeed, even appear in our central courtyard but had a garden and recreation place of their own. Foreign ways, it was frankly stated, could only endanger the perfect *tenue* [bearing, behavior] of the well-brought-up French girls.

The foreigners, on the other hand, a few of whom were not even pupils but only *pensionaires* boarding at the school while attending the Sorbonne or other universities, all had rooms of their own. And beyond seeing that we did not visit each other or leave the building unchaperoned, the school gave us no care of any kind. I was only fourteen at the time and in certain ways young for my age.

And now, on that first night, when Mademoiselle Pitou opened my door and lighted my single candle, I wished it might give a little more light.

It was a narrow and rather long room with dreadfully shadowy corners and deeply gleaming mirrors in which the little candle flame and all the dim objects repeated themselves strangely, as if seen through still water. Weirdly humped on the bed was a fat feather pouf in dark red sateen, and even the gargoyle snout of the tin hot-water jug beside the washstand had a disconcerting look. The long French window that opened on the court sagged away from its casement. In the draft that blew in under the door the draperies stirred queerly, and through the wide triangular crack between the door and the sill, I was to find later, mice scuttled and squeaked.

"Do not leave me, Mademoiselle Pitou!" Only I did not say it. She went out, closed the door behind her, opened it again to say, "Mind you aren't late for dinner," closed it again, and her heels clicked away down the stone passage.

But fear is close to fantasy and merges easily into dreams. People become used to it, even children, or perhaps especially children. I suppose among the many happy gifts of childhood there is none more precious than its relative unawareness of any but the fundamental physical states, its freedom from that constant preoccupation with physical ease, which comes later. At least that was my experience, and I cannot recall giving any thought whatever to the excruciating physical discomforts of the life that then began.

There was no central heat, of course, in the school. There were fireplaces or porcelain stoves in the common rooms, but there was no heat of any kind in the bedrooms. There was no light except severely rationed candles, no running water outside of the single toilet on each floor. Not a single bathtub in the entire building. The girls were marched from time to time to the public baths, but no money had been paid for me for extras. Night and morning, however, a maid put a tall tin jug of warm water outside my door, so I set the basin on the floor and washed as best I could.

I was ill-equipped with clothing and wore the same, summer and winter. But I don't remember ever asking myself whether I was warm or cold, comfortable or not. Children accept so much. Perhaps their spirits are still too new to the body to have become wholly one with it and at its mercy?

I was not late for dinner. Some twenty of us, of whom I was much the youngest, and one unexplained elderly French woman stood back of our chairs. We were in a long, low-ceilinged dining room with the floor running downhill. No windows, only doors opening onto the court. A white-globed gas lamp hung over the table. Nobody talked, although there were a few smiles and whispers. Across from each other in the narrow center of the table were two empty places.

At last, with the swing and rustle of full skirts that was part of the pattern and rhythm of the school, their hands clasped decorously over their stomachs, Mademoiselle Lemay and Mademoiselle Pitou swept in and to their places. Mademoiselle Lemay promptly closed her eyes, crossed herself and, without removing the half smile from her lean rosy face—the face of a fifteenth-century Spanish priest—rapidly spoke the blessing. Then she crossed herself again, saying "Au nom du père, du fils, du saint esprit, ainsi soit-il," and in the same breath, "Bon soir, madame," to the elderly lady beside her. Chairs scraped, we sat down, the maids appeared with the soup.

Hunger, I suppose, must be excluded from those discomforts to which children are more or less oblivious. Hunger is by no means so easily forgotten. And yet, between meals and when we were not actually in the presence of food, we did forget that too.

In that distant time all French food was good, at least in taste. Those subtle flavors, indeed, seemed a miracle to an unspoiled mid-American palate. And the bouquet arising from the thin leek soup served on my first night—little more than hot water flavored with a subtle blend of garden herbs, in which slices of bread were floating—was tantalizing and delicious. The meat dish was veal cooked with black olives. One paper-thin slice, I saw, was the portion to each person. And so complete was the discipline, so ingrained the idea of submission and propriety, that to think of taking two was inconceivable. Or if, with despair, one saw that the piece nearest one was even smaller than the other allotted portions, no one would dream of reaching for a larger one. And although the platter was passed a second time, no one helped herself.

That first night as on every other, each dish seemed only to stimulate your appetite and leave you almost breathless with hunger. Certain days were worse, for me at least, than others. The alternate Fridays, for instance, when we had eels cooked in brown sauce. Or the second and fourth Mondays that brought tripe. Or the appointed Saturdays on which, with painful inevitability, blood sausage made its appearance. I could swallow only a few mouthfuls of any of these dishes, and there was no substitute.

As I have said, I do not remember, between meals, thinking about how hungry I was. It was only with the food before you that you realized you could have eaten three times as much as the school's custom permitted you to put on your plate. Dessert brought on the most extreme suffering because there were good cakes and less good ones. The *religieuses* [cream puffs] were considered the prizes—and with what disguised anxiety all eyes watched the platter making the rounds, certain that nothing more thrilling than a ladyfinger would be left when it reached you.

---

2. The Other Foreign Students (Les Étrangères)

Carafes of red wine appeared on the table noon and night, and the custom was to pour an inch or two of it into the bottom of your glass and fill it up with water.

"Do you take wine?" the young girl beside me asked politely that first evening. Politely, too, she poured the proper amount, about two inches, into my tumbler and filled it with water. Something about her hand caught my attention. It was extremely supple and thin-fingered. Her body, noticeably small-waisted and full-breasted, had the same remarkable flexibility, and there was a peculiar grayish shadow under the olive tone of her ivory smooth skin.

"My name is Lucie Carrière," she went on. "We shall be neighbors at table so we must become acquainted." Her knowing dark eyes slanted a little under her delicate brows, and her voice had the slightly metallic resonance the French call *timbre*—a word for which I do not know an adequate English equivalent.

We immediately became the best of friends although I never saw her except at meals. She did not attend any of the classes I took, but it was from Lucie that I learned all the little I ever knew about the school. It was she who told me that intimacies between the girls were not encouraged or permitted. "Three girls may walk and talk together in the court if they do not do it too often, but never two alone," she advised me.

"But why?" I asked.

"Oh, you know." A little knowing smile appeared on her thin red lips. "They might recount all kinds of gossip, and besides that they might say things—bad things." She gave an amused laugh and glanced at Mademoiselle Lemay, of whom she was the special favorite.

I did not pursue the subject. After a moment she asked, "Where do you go on Saturday and Sunday?"

"Well, nowhere. Do you go away?"

"Oh, of course. I go to the house of my uncle in the Boulevard

Haussmann. On Saturday afternoon we go to the Concert Colonne where we are subscribed for a loge, and on Sunday we go to the Théâtre Français. Saturday night we eat in a restaurant, and Sunday night we have guests."

I wondered what they had to eat on Saturday night at the restaurant, and I imagined Lucie, her crinkly black hair all fluffed out and tied low, as the French fashion was then, with a ribbon bow, sitting very correct between her aunt and uncle in the box at the Concert Colonne or the Comédie Française.

Lucie was three-quarters French and one part Haitian Negro. Her grandfather had been governor of one of the French West Indian islands, and he had given his half-caste daughter—Lucie's mother—his name and an education in France. He also had supplied her with a sufficiently attractive dowry to ensure a good marriage, which she made by marrying into a colonial family. Lucie was one of the children of this match. Her French father, carrying on the traditions of his house, was at present in Haiti, and Lucie spent all her holidays with her French relatives in Paris. In every way my new friend, with her quiet, self-effacing voice, was the perfect *jeune fille* [young lady], behaving at every moment with the utmost propriety. I think too that she had never been made to feel at all ashamed of her heritage.

Lucie was fifteen, but she was already mature, a womanly little person, as mature perhaps as she would ever be. While on my other side at table sat a large, infantile Rumanian of the same age as Lucie but still a child. The others at our end of the table were older. There were two Russians, a Dane, a blond Norwegian with steady, honest eyes and a cautious mouth.

Next to her was the calamitous English girl, Ursula Watts, who was to cause me one of the great humiliations of my childhood. She was a repulsive individual with dank yellow hair, dull eyes, and an infuriatingly red nose. And beside Ursula sat a blond, shadowy young Pole of about twenty-six. She went to the Sorbonne, Lucie whispered. For six years the Pole had devoted herself exclusively to the study of the tracks left by snails in sand, convinced that in this slimy substance, at least according to my new friend, would be revealed the origins of matter.

By what colonial ramification of her family Lucie came to have a cousin hailing from the island of Madagascar I do not know, nor do I think she felt the slightest embarrassment when her unusually exotic cousin, Marianne, suddenly arrived in our midst from that far-off place.

One morning Lucie was excused from classes to go in the company of Mademoiselle Pitou to meet her cousin's train at the station. We were at table when they returned. They had taken off their wraps outside, and Marianne burst upon our attention bareheaded. On those winter days the gas lamps were always lighted in the dining room, and the brightness of the artificial light did nothing to diminish the effect of Marianne's hair.

To say that it was kinky is an understatement. Or even to call it hair. It was a flaring mass of something that looked like mattress stuffing, and it stood out half a foot on all sides around her head and was not only oiled with brilliantine but was sprinkled with a diamond-dustlike substance that used to appear on old-fashioned Christmas cards. Her skin was the color of a fine Havana cigar, her nose short with flared, mobile nostrils, and her liquid *mestizo* [mixed-blood] eyes—an off-shade of greenish amber—peered with a high, wild shining through a hedge of black lashes. Immense gold hoops swung merrily from her ears, and her red satin blouse glittered like a Christmas tree with embroidery of gold and silver sequins. Marianne's figure was a wild exaggeration of Lucie's. She was much taller, her waist and hips were even narrower and more flexible, and her superb high breasts were big as cantaloupes under the scarlet satin of her blouse.

Mademoiselle Lemay, who was presiding at our table as usual that noon, slowly moved her glance along the row of faces to where Marianne stood behind a chair and said, "Good morning, my child. Pray be seated." Marianne's wide mouth opened in a friendly smile, and she took her seat. Lucie, in her quiet way, had taken her seat beside me. She was excited by her cousin's arrival and apparently perfectly well pleased. She made some remark to Marianne about the lateness of the train, and Marianne, who in no way suffered from shyness, began to talk.

It was the first time I ever heard French spoken with the same accent with which the Negro people speak English, a surprise to me. Marianne, however, was not in appearance at all like the American Negroes. These, of course, derive from West African stock, whereas Madagascar lies off the east coast of Africa. There was more a similarity, it seems to me now, with the South Sea Islanders.

I never found that this exotic apparition made any special impression on anybody but me. Not even the diamond dust. To the French she was merely another foreigner, another *étrangère,* and if a little more strange than the rest of us, what of it? The Russians and Scandinavians and other continentals in our classes accepted her as she was without comment or surprise, a sign of the sophistication that was perhaps characteristic not only of France but of all Europe at that time, granting Marianne the right to be exactly as she was and as different from themselves as they were from her.

Marianne, however, did not stay with us long. She was an extremely nice person, friendly, well-mannered, and liked by everybody. But she never came close to any of us except Lucie. After every meal they would go off together arm in arm, the rule that no two girls should be alone together having been suspended for them as it would have been for sisters.

Then all at once Marianne was no longer there, and I do not remember asking myself why or what became of her. We must have got used to her soon, although she never mitigated in any way the unusual details of her appearance, nor was she asked to do so by the authorities. The diamond dust still sprinkled in her hair, the gold hoops always swung in her ears, and her smell of temple incense gave a strange accent to the aroma of garlic and Brussels sprouts seldom absent from the dining room. We talked to her, and she talked to us, words that all understood, but there was no point of contact. And when after a few weeks she disappeared it was as if she had never been there at all.

---

3. Regimen of the School

The winter sun in Paris rises late, and it was always dark when we got up. It was easiest to do everything very fast. Uncoil yourself from a tight knot under the red pouf, put out a reluctant hand to light the candle, then bound across the icy tiles, snatch open the door, bring in the jug of warm water and wash, rather sketchily, I fear, and dress under the shelter of a cotton flannel nightgown.

Shivering and rubbing their hands, the girls poured into the dining room. Though the gaslights whistled rather cheerily, your breath was visible in the air like the steam that rose from the pitchers of hot chocolate and café au lait set out on the tables. Chocolate was preferred in spite of the fact that it was often scorched and only tasted of chocolate if you got what was near the bottom of the pitcher. A bowl and spoon were at each place, and there were always baskets of fresh rolls. None of the demoiselles was present in the morning, so you could sit where you chose.

Classes with Mademoiselle Pitou began in a frigid, ink-stained little room at nine o'clock. There all morning we studied French grammar and wrote in French from dictation. I knew French perfectly then, the way a child knows it. I had studied nothing else for the two or three years before leaving America and had had six months of schooling in France before arriving at the convent.

In the afternoons we studied literature and history with Mademoiselle Boileau, whose point of view was startlingly limited. We learned that the kings of France had been almost all heroic and sainted men, that the power, glory, genius, virtue, and achievement of the world were exclusively French and Catholic, and that the present republic was a godless institution that could not last. Our geographies and history books referred to all persons and places outside the Catholic world as heathen.

This approach to education reduced the field of inquiry considerably and the amount of information it was necessary to learn. Even French subjects were simplified by numerous omissions. Voltaire, for example, rated just one line in a footnote, and Arouét was a writer of inferior talent and an infidel.

At four o'clock I practiced my violin for an hour. There was a series of small rooms along the court in each of which was a piano and from which at all hours came scales and trills and five-finger exercises and a good deal of Chaminade, a French composer whose music was then much in vogue. The pupil who used the room after me was the Rumanian girl, Octavia Pompiliano. I was supposed to leave, of course, the instant she arrived, but she always came a few moments early and begged me to stay for a little while. She wanted to talk about home.

After dinner the older girls went to their rooms, and the rest of us were shepherded by Mademoiselle Pitou into the Salle d'Études, the small salon reserved for study during the after-dinner hours. There we sat for an hour or two in a small study that gave on the trembling, distantly roaring street, hearing the muted roar of the big vans passing close to the small casement windows, tightly closed with wooden shutters and set securely behind a lattice of iron bars. I am sure those windows had never been opened. To the pervading school smell of breathed-over air, coal gas, and old flesh, in that room something else was added: the steamy, subterranean effluvia of cellars, mold, and rats—the smell of an old city.

Talking in the Salle d'Études was not permitted. We sat on straight chairs drawn up around a center table under the inevitable whistling gas lamp. Mademoiselle Pitou's steel knitting needles clicked defiantly over the noise of the street.

But if it seems to you that an evening spent in the Salle d'Études was something less than agreeable, you would be wrong. Against the rules, not too severely enforced at this hour, there would be whispers, jokes that, because of the repression, assumed fabulous proportions, became so sidesplitting that they threw us, particularly the overgrown, childish Rumanian girl, Octavia Pompiliano, into agonies of suppressed mirth. The room was bright, it was relatively warm—less from the fire that smoldered meagerly on the hearth and occasionally threw a puff of milky blue and yellow smoke into the room—than from our own bodies. And the lopsided walls, the crooked ceiling, the look the room had of being crushed a little out of shape by the weight of the years, seemed to bring close about one human life and warmth.

———————

4. Hierarchies of the School

There were, I quickly gathered, hierarchies among the directresses or *demoiselles* of the school, with Mademoiselle de Vaugirard and a person called Mademoiselle Laroque at the top and Mademoiselle Pitou and others at the bottom. Mademoiselle Lemay was well up but not in the highest rank.

Mademoiselle Pitou was in the lowest rank and was also the most unwashed. She was a small woman, and for all her pudding face and dumpy, corseted body and little eyes like black currants poked deep into suet, and for all her kindliness too, there was also a kind of needle sharpness about her. Her little, twinkly eyes were needle-bright and saw nothing important but all the tiny details the way an insect's eyes must.

Mademoiselle Armand, the school's housekeeper, *charged*, in the French phrase, with the *matériel* [furnishings and equipment], was therefore treated as an inferior. She was far below the heights of such women as Mademoiselle de Vaugirard or Mademoiselle Laroque. But I fancy Mademoiselle Armand was the kindest and most normal of all the women there. She was a big, robust woman with shiny, rather stupid pop-eyes. If it had been in her power, I am sure she would have supplied a little more food to the ravenously hungry foreign girls.

---

5. Octavia

The Rumanian girl who often chatted with me after my violin practice, Octavia Pompiliano, was oppressively big and puppyish. She frisked and bounced like a huge awkward puppy that always wants to put his paws on your shoulders and knock you down. I did not find her interesting. She talked with a lisp and wrapped all the crisp French syllables in cotton wool, and it was always about her brother in military school, her mama and papa, and their big house in Bucharest that she wanted to confide.

"Rumania," she never failed to assure me proudly, "is not Germanic and it is not Slav. It is Roman. I, for example, am pure Roman. But absolutely pure."

Nor was that hard to believe. For you have seen her big classic face with the sculptural lips, strong straight nose springing directly from the forehead, with well-set but rather empty eyes on countless monuments—especially those representing the sturdier virtues or such concepts as freedom, law, and victory in war. Her countenance could be seen on monuments too that are slightly pocked by the weather, for Octavia's skin suffered, rather more than most, from the blemishes of adolescence.

She did, however, have a real talent for the piano, and sometimes we got permission to practice together. I had a book of violin and piano sonatas, and we always ended up with Rumanian and gypsy airs out of her memory. This innocent occupation, however, was eventually to bring down upon us the awful disaster of Ursula Watts. But that was later.

It was during one of these practice hours that Mademoiselle Pitou burst in upon us in a state of subdued excitement. We were not playing that day but were engaged in a supposedly guilty tête à tête and thought she had come to scold. But she was much too preoccupied even to see. It was Mademoiselle de Vaugirard, she said. At last she had indicated that I must be brought and presented to her.

"And, my little American miss, one doesn't keep Mademoiselle de Vaugirard waiting, so run fast and wash your hands."

---

6. Mademoiselle de Vaugirard

I should like to have seen Lucie's cousin Marianne meeting in that gothic chamber above the dining room with Mademoiselle de Vaugirard, the school's almost sanctified authority figure and the most completely stylized person I have ever seen. I see her sitting in her handsome fauteuil upholstered in its authentic Utrecht velvet, among the tapestries, the paintings and carvings of the martyrs, the signed photos of the Roman prelates and the pope, giving her studied smile of welcome to this dusky East African princess whose white blood had taken away so little of her swift jungle grace and primitive aliveness.

Mademoiselle de Vaugirard was as stylized as a Louis Quinze [XV] chair, as a château. Stylized in the way she composed her features or the way she pronounced her words, moved her lips, carried her head, or in the brisk professional way she spoke that was almost automatic, leaving her brain free for all the Jesuitical machinations with which, one always felt—perhaps quite wrongly—it was constantly concerned.

That was the way I remembered Mademoiselle de Vaugirard after meeting her for the first time following a midnight Mass. She had put out her hand and had drawn me close to implant a ghostly kiss first on one cheek, then on the other. Standing this way with my face about on a level with hers, I could see no blemish in the narcissus-petal purity of her white skin or on her dazzling teeth.

"So here we are, little-American-girl-among-strangers. And the smallest of them all. They have spoken to me about you, and I hear that you are a good girl. Well, well, well. Uzushzzz . . . "

I found now that this inhalation, like the indrawn breath of the Japanese, served the practical purpose of reversing the fine spray that flew in all directions when Mademoiselle de Vaugirard spoke.

Then, to my surprise, she had begun to speak in English, accurately but with an extremely strong accent, coughing up the h-sounds from the bottom of her throat. "And how are you getting along here? Are you happy? Do you apply yourself to your studies?"

But her words, whether French or English, like her smile, had no relation to anything, were as without personal meaning, as stylized, for example, as the gestures of a dancer in the minuet. You knew that the flow of her real thoughts, intent on the business of her great enterprise, was not interrupted by the smallest ripple.

Her room itself was strange. It was as if a busy businesswoman had moved her desk and account books into a corner of the Cluny Museum. Long, deeply recessed windows went from floor to ceiling, but close against the panes were stone walls, as if the rest of the building had grown up about this ancient core. And they were splendidly hung with rotting but brilliant emerald velvet worked in gold with armorial bearings. The gaslight, greenish-white through the Welsbach mantles of the lamps, fell upon the most incongruous objects—the thronelike chair on which she sat, the hideous brass-trimmed Franklin stove, on dark tapestries and filing cases, on an iron safe and an ivory Christ agonizing on a life-sized cross.

For a moment longer she carried on the routine of her job. Where had I learned to speak French? Was I unfortunate enough to be a little Protestant? Had I any brothers and sisters over there in America?

"And so, au revoir, my child. Apply yourself well. Uzushzzz . . . " she said, drawing in again the flecks of foam that 'til then had been sprinkling my face.

---

7. Mademoiselle Laroque

"And so today you will see her," Lucie remarked, looking at me with her sly, teasing expression. "Are you curious? Are you excited?"

"Well, if it was Mademoiselle de Vaugirard . . . " I began.

"Ah, that is different altogether. Mademoiselle de Vaugirard is something nobody sees except at a distance like the sun and moon. But Mademoiselle Laroque is not like that. In fact, it sometimes happens—it might happen," she added rather mysteriously, "that you saw a great deal of her indeed."

We were all in our places in the dining room, waiting. Even Mademoiselle Lemay was there in the place Mademoiselle Pitou had occupied the night before. And when at last Mademoiselle Laroque swept in I would have known, even if Lucie had never spoken of her at all, that her presence at once changed everything. It was a different room, and we were different people.

What was it actually that one saw? A tall dark-haired woman nearing middle age, with an air of authority and a kind of fierce pride. Mademoiselle Laroque was dressed as they all were in the costume of the demoiselles but without the knitted cape. Her soft brown hair was parted in the middle and set low, but on the top of her head was a shining psyche knot. She was handsome too, with a slight resemblance to Dante on her strong face. And part of the excitement she brought into the room was a sense of ease and worldliness, of drawing rooms and palaces.

She went to her place without looking up and, crossing herself, asked the blessing rapidly and bowed to the old lady beside her. Then, suddenly, her gravity gave way, and, holding her head high, she scanned the table with a faintly mocking smile and said, "Well, Mesdemoiselles, I wish you all a good day."

"Good day, Mademoiselle Laroque," the table answered eagerly. All, that is, but one. The eyes of the Norwegian girl remained stubbornly lowered, and her lips did not move.

Suddenly I realized Mademoiselle Laroque was speaking to me.

"Eh, bien, ma petite Grace, racontez nous un petit peu ce que c'est l'Amérique. Vous venez de bien loin. [Well, little Grace, tell us what America is like. You come from far away.]"

"Yes, Mademoiselle."

"And tell me, please, what part of that great country do you come from?"

"From St. Paul, Minnesota, Mademoiselle. It is on the Mississippi River."

"But I can't believe it. It is too good to be possible." She put back her fine head and laughed a throaty, rippling, contagious laugh. "All my life, even as a little child, I saw in the geographies that word 'Mississippi.' It seemed stranger to me than the Nile or the Amazon or even the Congo. 'The Mississippi' . . . and never did I expect to see a native from that remote place. Tell us, then, a little about it. What is it like?"

Mademoiselle Laroque. How often have I wondered what strange genius animated and afterward ruined that fascinating woman. By what perversity of fate had she come to enter a celibate order, to live a narrow life immured in that musty, ancient, medieval place, ringed round with ideas and conventions more fantastically medieval than the worn stone flags of the stairways and halls? What fiery dignity she had, and what humor and verve and a kind of debonair realism there was in the way she spoke, held her head. What an adult person she was, holding in herself the potent charm both of a woman and a man.

And what special hell she raised in the name of God in that fusty, straightlaced, unaired community of women, where long shirts must carefully hide any suggestion of femininity, where one must speak low, hold one's elbows close, never under any circumstance cross one's legs—to cross one's legs would have been as improper as standing on one's head—one must compose one's features, keep one's eyes straight ahead . . .

When Mademoiselle Laroque sat at our table, the light shining from above brought out the down-drawn Dante-esque shadows, the aquilinity of her nose. And yet she was beautiful. Or was it the magnetism of her fire and pride and gaiety and sureness of herself that gave the illusion of beauty? In her laughing dark eyes there was always that shaft of irony. But her rallying was without rudeness, and her making of these young women kittens to be played with had an adult quality that made, of whomever she selected to address, a pet to be buffeted lightly and with affection.

Mademoiselle Laroque came to our table several times a week. When she was there she addressed most of her remarks to me. Her tone was at once bantering and tender and ironical, and my replies would bring forth peals of her rich, contagious laughter. To be singled out in this way restored to me a natural status. I had always been the center of attention in our family, and what more proper than that I should be here?

But there was more to it than that. In spite of the vast difference in age, race, and every kind of experience, intellectually we were conditioned to the same atmosphere, we had the same love of a certain turn of thought, a certain quickness and gusto that were identical, we laughed at the same things in the same way. In the security and privilege and freedom I felt with her she might easily have been my mother . . . or perhaps my father, as there was in her a curious blend of man and woman.

After meals we would crowd around her, not all of us, but those who seemed to revolve within her orbit, and she would stand, with her hand usually on my shoulder, chatting with us a few moments.

I remember the first occasion on which we were alone together. It was in the dining room after luncheon. I had been among the girls surrounding her, and then, all at once they were gone and we were alone. The maids had cleared the table and spread it with the red baize cover. Fog stood white as cotton at the glass doors, the gas lamps whistled cozily.

She drew me down onto a small chair beside hers. "Tell me, my child, have no orders been left for you to be taken to your church?"

"My father doesn't believe in church," I replied promptly." He thinks it's all nonsense."

Her eyes widened with surprise, and then she burst out laughing. "No, but truly! So that is what your father says? And he is quite right as a matter of fact, so far as his church is concerned."

Pleased with my success I began to favor her with some of his arguments, of which I had an unlimited supply. "He says they tell you God is an all-merciful and loving father, and in the next breath that He roasts His poor children in Hell for all eternity. He says the wickedest human father wouldn't do that."

She suddenly became grave. "My poor child, those are foolish arguments. It all comes because Protestants try to think for themselves. True religion is too great for that."

I was happy to be there beside her. It didn't matter what she talked about. To be near her was to be home, to feel her affection flowing about me and encircling me, like the arms of a beloved parent. Home, home and loved again! My heart was so full of happiness and light and gaiety I could have pranced and bounded like a colt or a lamb in spring.

But I had to sit still and listen. Well, that was the next best thing. If she wanted to talk about religion, let her. It was a subject I had heard discussed—no, not discussed, since no one in our household with the possible exception of myself ever dared to contradict my father, but lectured upon by him—ever since I could talk.

Mademoiselle Laroque brought up the subject of Martin Luther and Henry VIII and made them sound discreditable indeed to the cause of Protestantism, a monk who wanted to get married and a king who wanted to get divorced. Protestant sects were many; Catholicism was one sect. Truth was one, and therefore Catholicism was truth. And there was something about the tablecloth.

"We see that that tablecloth is all red, therefore it cannot be all green or all purple."

I didn't care about the tablecloth or Henry VIII. Nothing she said as yet had caught my attention, but to be there beside her, selected out of all the rest to receive her undivided attention, that filled me with joy.

At last she brought the interview to an end and stood looking down, laughing again, her teeth milky white against her dark skin.

"Little by little, n'est-ce pas, little Grace?" She put her two hands on my face and, lifting it to hers, kissed my cheeks and my lips.

Suddenly I remembered my history lesson, which I had missed. "Oh, that will be all right, I think. Don't bother. I will explain," she assured me.

Once or twice each week Mademoiselle Laroque presided at our table, and often afterward I would find myself alone with her. Then the empty dining room, smelling of soap and crumbs, broccoli and floor polish, became a kind of no-man's-land having no relation to the ordinary functions of the school but dedicated to this friendship that was so genuine and yet so full too of a subtle excitement and the sense of something mysterious and unknown.

The words Mademoiselle Laroque spoke to me still seemed unimportant. She continued to touch on Martin Luther and Henry VIII, on the oneness of truth, the divine origins of the Roman Catholic Church. I had had a long and precocious experience with such dialectics, and I found it dull and unconvincing.

On the other hand, gradually too, I was beginning in memory and feeling to associate Mademoiselle Laroque with the dim, strange beauty of the ancient churches. It began to seem to me I had visited them with her. That she had put my hand in the font of holy water, that I had made the sign of the cross, that with her, I had knelt in front of the small crimson lamb, swaying slightly on his long chain before the altar.

This association became so real that I could no longer distinguish the truth. I could no longer have said positively that it was not so, so that I actually, finally, believed it. I did not believe it with my mind, but in some other part of me I did. Nor did I try not to believe. It became extremely painful and confusing to try to argue with myself. Indeed, my memory of Mademoiselle Laroque's presence beside me at those times was more real to me than much of what happened about me at school. Or rather, I lived two lives that scarcely touched, the life of the classes, my chats at lunch and dinner with Lucie and the ordinary life of the school, and this emotional dream.

---

8. The Christmas Play

The great event of the holiday season was that I had been chosen to play a leading role in the Christmas play. All the other actors were

French, the French girls we never met and only saw at a distance, sleek and demure, their long hair beautifully cared for, their clothes showing the effect of attention received at not too distant homes. Compared to them, we *étrangères,* far from our families, looked after by nobody, must have been a tousled, sorry-looking lot.

But one day Lucie demanded, "What did I tell you? What did I say?" She smiled at me with a glint of friendly malice in her slanted dark eyes. "I told you you'd be the next pet and now you are. Have you heard the news?"

"What news?"

"Not about the play?"

I shook my head.

"Why, you're going to have a role in the Christmas play. Mademoiselle Laroque directs it, and that proves that you're the pet, as I said you'd be. Foreign girls never act in the Christmas play."

As always, Lucie, who got all the news before anybody else, was right. Mademoiselle Laroque announced it at lunch. That very day we read our parts, and I was cast in the play.

The theatre was a real theatre. It was in the new wing of the old building, underneath the chapel. There was a fine stage with wings and footlights and a curtain, a small orchestra recruited among the pupils, and what seemed to me a vast auditorium out in front.

Of the performance itself I am ashamed to say I remember nothing but myself, the beautiful trailing gown I wore with a jeweled belt, the red on my cheeks, and below the bright barrier of the footlights the darkness in which sat the audience whose faces—pink discs—were like even rows of cabbages in a garden.

I remember my own voice and the somber reverberation of the

lines: "C'était pendant l'horreur d'une profonde nuit que ma mère Jezebel devant moi apparu . . . [It was during the horror of a dark night that my mother Jezebel appeared before me . . .]."

I must admit that I have always liked big rumbling passages if they were turned out by a master, the so-called purple passages. And the protagonists of the one-syllable school forget how often the masters did turn them out, from Homer and Aeschylus to Shakespeare, Wordsworth, and Keats to Francis Thompson.

Then as always it was only when acting the role of someone else that I felt in the least like myself. Confident and complete. And I learned that it was the acting in the play itself that was the high moment, its own reward.

Afterwards the compliments of the elegant French mothers and fathers, the gloved hands, the brilliantined beards, the smell of perfume, of furs, the tiny veils, the musical inflection of the Parisian speech when they sometimes bent down to kiss in the perfunctory French way the two cheeks of the "petite américaine qui a si bien joué en Français . . . [the little American girl who has played her part in French so well]"—all that was an ebb in the great tide of joy it had been to live for an hour in the splendid world of the imaginary life.

That holiday week was marked by several other remarkable happenings. Both Christmas and New Year's Eve we stayed up 'til midnight to attend Mass. The school was more or less empty, which added to its charm, for all those who had families or friends left after the Christmas play and did not return until after the holidays.

I did not leave. My mother and sister were in Florence, and they forgot to write or even to send me a Christmas present. I received no letters or presents, but I did stay up for midnight Mass and above all for the supper that came afterwards.

Christmas was marked for me only by the delirious experience of eating supper in the middle of the night. It was necessary, of course, to go to midnight Mass first, and aside from the pleasure of wearing a black veil loaned for the occasion by Mademoiselle Pitou, I found that a boring interlude. It was the fault of the chapel: it was too new, too bright, too cheery, and too denuded of mystery. I knew only the old churches, those dim, gray places where the light lost itself upwards into the shaped darkness of towers, infinitely high above, and where in the twilight far below one walked, small and close to the death-cold floor of stone.

The service on Christmas Eve, of which I understood nothing, seemed endless. I became hideously sleepy, and nothing but the reports of what would be for supper kept me awake or alive.

But finally it was over, and we were out in the cold air with the sparse, slow snowflakes falling bright before the lighted windows of the courtyard. I was wide awake again.

In the dining room the table was set with clean linen, and in place of the carafes of red wine set at intervals along the table were old dusty black bottles, wearing the insignia of cobwebs.

How wide the knowledge and tradition of good living was in France when even the cook of a grubby school like ours could turn out, as she had, a flawless supper! There was a dark consommé garnished with delicate marrow balls, a *Vol au Vent financière,* a green salade of watercress and romaine, and—my favorite—*a purée of marrons* [chestnut pudding], flavored with vanilla and covered with clotted cream.

It could not have been more exquisitely prepared. And out of the old bottles, dimly labeled, was poured for each of us a little wine—no water added—so ruby red and clear that it was like a liquid jewel shining in the delicate glasses. I do not know if it was this night or on New Year's Eve, when there was another midnight Mass and another supper, that we were honored by the presence of Mademoiselle de Vaugirard. To one of these feasts she brought her teeth, her smile, and her casual, dominating, rather royal manner.

I have never from any woman received an impression of greater ability of a certain kind than I did from Mademoiselle de Vaugirard. She was a power both in Paris and in Rome, and one did not need to be told it, one had only to be in her presence. And yet I never heard her utter anything but the most banal remarks repeated so mechanically she scarcely seemed aware that she was saying them at all.

But the essence of individuals is never found, of course, in what they say. Or their personal worth to be gauged by any purely verbal expression they make of principles. And how long it takes some people to learn this! How many never learn it at all!

---

9. Religious Instruction Continues

It was a black January of slashing rains or bitter frozen fog. We existed in perpetual twilight, under perpetually falling water. I was always cold but never caught cold; nor did I suffer from the chilblains that were almost universal in the school.

Emotionally I lived in Mademoiselle Laroque. Almost always when she presided at our table she would linger afterwards for a little talk with me, and always the talk was about religion. As yet she confined herself to reasoning, which seemed to me even then rather puerile and not worth considering. I had heard too much reasoning on the subject already, but for the joy of being with her I am afraid I pretended an interest I did not feel.

Then a day came when Mademoiselle Laroque said impatiently, "But one is not at ease in this room. It is too public. One does not know at what moment there will be some ridiculous interruption. I think next week, my child, I will find time to meet you upstairs in the grand salon."

The following Wednesday she gave me rendezvous in the grand salon on the second floor. Three o'clock, she had said.

There had been only half a dozen of us at table that noon, and now I took myself through what seemed like a deserted school. There was no light in the corridor, and it had such a worn and dented floor that the whole effect was like the corridor one sometimes walks through with a shudder in ancient prisons.

I had never seen the grand salon in the daytime as it was only used for the school's Sunday evening receptions. There was little light in the huge room by day, and all the immense mirrors, gray and shining like water, were filled with the twilight, the shadows, as it were, the stillness of that expectant, empty place.

The grand salon was an immense space, divided in the middle but so low-ceilinged that it lost the impression to some extent of great size. The beautiful, worn parquetry floor was bare of rugs and so slippery you crossed it with a skating motion to keep your balance. Along the front wall French windows crazily set in the deeply settled wall gave on the narrow, ancient street below. The chairs were upholstered in crimson with gilt and ebony frames. They were ranged side by side all around the walls, with a throne for Mademoiselle de Vaugirard and an armchair here and there for the demoiselles who, on Sunday evenings, would be dispersed among the pupils. Crystal chandeliers hung from the ceiling, and candelabra with wax candles stood on the mantle pieces, with false ones along the walls.

I sat down on a small chair in the corner by the door. Sometimes the room shook to the rumble of the passing buses, and sometimes the floors and the old walls made small creakings, seeming to move like old rheumatic joints and to sigh.

Then I heard the familiar swish and whisper of long skirts in the corridor and the sound of her quick, firm step. Mademoiselle Laroque came in quickly, closing the rolling doors behind her. She looked tall and handsome standing there, her grave face yielding to its sudden ironic smile and a kind of mocking tender laughter lighting up her dark eyes. "And so here we are, my dear little child," she began.

I had the impulse to kneel and pray, to lift up my eyes in ecstasy, to cross myself with holy water, to enter a confessional booth and confess mysteriously to an unseen priest about the perplexities and vague anguish that at times beset even a child's heart—to express a whole nameless category of emotion with which Mademoiselle Laroque was now deeply involved.

Holding my two hands in hers she spoke rather rapidly about the authentic origins of the Catholic Church and touched again on the far-from-creditable origins of the Protestant churches.

Suddenly I found her looking at me expectantly, and seeing that some remark was expected of me, I said something about the Spanish Inquisition. I remarked that my father had always considered it somewhat discreditable that a Christian church had supported a most un-Christian institution.

"Ah, but an institution cannot be blamed for the wrongdoing of individuals," she retorted. "Human nature is feeble and prone to error. No blame for its sins can be laid at the door of the church. That has nothing to do with the infallibility of the church itself."

It crossed my mind that the sins of Martin Luther and Henry VIII seemed to have borne heavily against Protestantism, but I was not interested enough to speak of it and said nothing more.

She was smiling again, her brows lifted, and she was looking down at me through half-closed lids. "Come then, my child. Shall we say next Wednesday then? It is time for me to go on my walk outdoors."

This suggestion that it was her habit to walk in the garden was the only glimpse I ever had of her personal life. I wished she would tell me more, what part of France she came from, why she had done what she did. I have since wondered where, in what woods, and by what sea Mademoiselle Laroque walked in the twilight. But these demoiselles, like other nuns—if indeed they were nuns—never spoke of the past.

She had ceased speaking now, and I realized that the brief lecture was finished. She was so beautiful that I wanted to fling my arms around her neck and hug her the way I used to hug them all at home, going the rounds of the sitting room at bedtime, dragging it out, postponing to the last possible moment the horrid departure up the stairs, knowing myself to be the pet, feeling all about me their love and limitless indulgence.

But to hug Mademoiselle Laroque seemed too familiar, treating her as I had my Aunt Lizzie, who used always to say, "Hug me tight, Baby, squeeze hard." I hadn't thought about Aunt Lizzie or my father or any of them for a long time. Children succeed so wonderfully in not thinking of what will cause them pain. But now, with this loving and, as I thought, maternal woman beside me, I dared remember them.

"Such a little dear," she murmured, "a little one I could love."

I had at last put my head on her shoulder, and she stroked my cheek with her strong, not supple hand with the thick, pointed fingers that always hung curved in a little, like claws. Then she lifted my face to hers and kissed my cheeks and my eyes and my mouth.

But now the kisses no longer reminded me of home. All the memories of my family retreated again into the hidden place where they could bring me no pain, and I wanted to go away. We parted without speaking further.

---

10. The Concert

Among the school events that first winter there occurred one that even now causes me a kind of fury to set down. This dreadful occasion is printed as ineffably upon my memory as a hieroglyphic on stone. Because of her talent for the piano, Octavia, another of the *étrangères*, became involved with me in the ghastly affair of Ursula Watts.

The first Sunday night of every month was a gala occasion. The entire school assembled for music and recitations in the grand salon above the small salon where we studied in the evenings. After the performance a small cup of hot chocolate and a confection called a *petit beurre* were served.

Foreign girls seldom took part in the actual programs of the school, but now one of the demoiselles—and because of its utter ineptitude I suspect it must have been Mademoiselle Pitou—conceived a disastrous idea. At one of the Sunday soirées in the grand salon, Octavia and I were to perform jointly with Ursula Watts.

This odious girl was taking singing lessons, and Octavia and I had sometimes held our breath when we heard her raucous and unmusical voice, always elaborately off key, being exercised in an adjoining cubicle. It was not a voice at all in any relation that word has to song, but an indescribable tuneless screech.

I am sure that if we had been French girls this thing could not have happened, but that it did happen was a sign of the carelessness with which foreign girls were for the most part regarded. Not being French we were not entirely human. If, for example, a trained dog had been taught to sing one would not be critical, one would simply be interested at how near he could come to reproducing the human voice.

Or perhaps I am wrong. Perhaps it was Ursula herself who suggested the trio. At any rate the order was issued that Octavia, Ursula, and I should render the "Berceuse de Jocelyn" at the forthcoming Sunday salon. Octavia was to accompany Ursula on the piano, and I was to play the violin obligato. The news that not one but three foreigners were to perform caused a slight ripple throughout the school. At our table in the dining room the Polish girl, who was said never to speak, had begun of late to exchange a few remarks with me. As we finished supper she remarked, "I have never attended one of the salons, but I shall this evening. I have confidence in you." Alas.

Promptly at eight o'clock the French girls, neatly and elegantly dressed, their shining hair hanging loose halfway down their backs and caught there by a ribbon bow, filed in accompanied by their teachers. We, the *étrangères,* followed, shepherded by Mademoiselle Pitou and

Mademoiselle Boileau. Stiff chairs were ranged around the walls, and we sat down, heads up, elbows in, feet together and properly placed on the floor.

The school was out in full force, and Mademoiselle de Vaugirard made an impressive, smiling entrance, even sending a benevolent flash from her big golden eyes in our direction. We rose in a body.

"Good evening, my dear children. Well, well, well, excellent . . . excellent . . . ushsuzzz . . . Be seated, I pray, mais oui, mais oui, mais oui . . . "

What a display of teeth! What an elegant stiff dress of heavy black faille silk with a gold pin at the throat! When Mademoiselle de Vaugirard took her seat on the thronelike chair reserved for her, we all sat down. The whisper of skirts subsided into the silence that follows the settling of a flock of birds.

When all was quiet Mademoiselle Pitou, in her crisp, trilling Provençale accent, announced our names, nationalities, and the fact that we would render the "Berceuse de Jocelyn." I had at that time an excellent Kootz violin, and my playing, such as it was, had always been made a good deal of. I felt no self-consciousness at performing.

We took our places about the grand piano, the a-note was sounded, the strings properly tightened, the audience assumed expressions of polite anticipation, and Octavia sounded off. I joined in with the bars that preceded the song. Then in her tuneless squeak and unspeakable French accent Ursula began to intone the melody. Except for the fact that Ursula seemed to be singing in an entirely different key we were at least all three together.

But then something happened. I think Ursula turned two pages instead of one, and suddenly while Octavia and I were playing the verse, Ursula seemed to be in the middle of the refrain. The effect on the audience was at first startling, then excruciatingly funny. Irrepressible smiles tore at rigidly stiffened lips. Shoulders shook with chokingly stifled laughter.

Octavia and I had now located Ursula, but we had no sooner fallen in with her than she, with an apologetic and imbecile giggle, perceived that she had skipped something and went back to the place where she thought she had left off. But it was somewhere else. We weren't sure where. I decided on one spot, Octavia on another, and Ursula went on quite independently of everybody.

Desperately I saw Mademoiselle Laroque's excruciatingly amused smile, saw her shaking her head, put her two hands over her ears, saw the Polish girl, seated near the door, rise like a dark shadow and vanish from sight.

Why I didn't stop playing I cannot imagine. But I didn't. I suppose it was partly sheer panic and partly the discipline of finishing what you had started. But then Octavia wouldn't stay put. She began plunging about in an effort to find where Ursula was, hoping that by skipping here and there she would eventually be where Ursula was. But she never was.

We played on doggedly to the bitter end with a piano and violin obligato that seldom had any relation either to the song, the singer, or to each other.

I've read a good deal about the repression of painful thoughts into the unconscious, and the phrase never means much until one looks back at the happenings of one's own childhood. Then one realizes that it does happen. The rage, the shame, and what seemed the eternal humiliation I had suffered were before the next day successfully tucked away out of reach. I had thought when I rushed out of the salon without waiting for Mademoiselle de Vaugirard's smile and her "ushsuzzz" and her "bon soir" that I would never again draw a happy breath. The next morning it was almost as if it had never happened. I simply did not think of it then or for many years afterward.

---

11. The School and Its Garden in Spring

The buildings now included in the school had been put up in different centuries and were of different types. The oldest were the rooms about the central stairwell that was said to go back to the twelfth century—which it may have done.

The wing that housed the dormitories used by the French students and the classrooms was of a more elegant type. The ceilings were high, with handsome cornices and fine walnut paneling. It might have been an eighteenth-century hotel or townhouse, and the room in which algebra class was taught might once have been a small library or one of the more intimate living rooms. It was of beautiful proportions with fine paneling and fine hand-carved doors in some natural-colored wood—walnut, I suppose—and a curved ceiling touched here and there with gold. And the garden into which it looked remains the essence of what to me is France and, especially, Paris.

It was a green garden. I do not remember that a single flower grew there except, in the spring, white and purple lilacs. The garden was hidden behind the immensely high wall enclosing it, shutting it off from the rest of the school grounds. Water dripped everywhere and ivy grew dark on the gray stone. Among the trees and ancient shrubs—so old their trunks were like tree trunks, gnarled among their shiny dark laurel leaves—were water-pocked statuettes of nymphs and cupids and satyrs, half-effaced, and in the wall were set carved panels before which small fountains played.

As the suggestion is always more powerful than the completed statement, the spring can be all the more poignant for seeing little of it. It came with that softness that it seems to bring only to France at Eastertime, and the smell and sense of it reached over our walls, through our occasionally opened doors, into our musty rooms, freshening that smell of old wood, old stone, old flesh. The pointed white and purple spears of the lilacs among the green in that hidden, dripping garden, their fragrance blown into the beautiful eighteenth-century, nobly proportioned, walnut-paneled room, the open windows bringing in the incredibly soft air, the misty green of the four plane trees in the courtyard: that was all I saw of it.

As spring began the mist that drifted about the garden seemed faintly lavender, and there was an indescribable quickening. The quality of light changed, there was a faintly bluish color in the air, and the sunlight that penetrated for an hour or so in the afternoon on the violently green grass was yellow as a banana peel with an overtone that turned the shadows blue.

Here in the garden too, the ladies walked, French ladies who had come to this school when they were girls and who made their retreat here each spring. Quietly strolling at certain hours, the women walked under the trees along the wet paths where water trickled brightly, bridging in some way that schizophrenic gap between life and point of view as a *jeune fille* in a school like this and the life of a French woman of the world, married to a Frenchman and moving in Parisian society. What an accommodating creature the human animal is!

Sometimes they looked sad, sometimes not, but always they were elegantly dressed in a quiet way, and always—and there is a perfect French word for it—*recueillies*. Drawn into themselves, turning deep into their hearts and consciousness, seeking to reenter themselves.

Sometimes a priest or two walked here. But I never saw the French girls or the demoiselles. The latter had their own garden walled away from this one. This was France, the French way, privacy fiercely guarded, formal walks, clipped borders, high walls, time when one must be *recueillies*—and elegantly dressed. And Paris to me is gray stone, a green place behind high walls, mist among green trees, water dripping against gray stone, the shapes of ancient gods, neglected and timeworn, giving classic shapes to the groves and *allées*.

---

12. Easter

Easter came, and again the school emptied for the vacation. Even the foreign girls had left for the most part, as plans had been made for them to visit friends or make chaperoned excursions. Mademoiselle Laroque had departed triumphantly for Rome with a group of girls who were to visit the monuments and be presented to the pope.

It was an early spring and hot. I never left the school. No provision had been made for that. Apparently my pension was paid and not a penny more. No money was ever sent to me.

---

13. A Miracle

The time did not pass quickly at school. It seemed to stand still. Then, suddenly, the students were all back, classes were resumed, and everything went on as usual except that suddenly a miracle happened.

It was a Sunday in May and everything a day in May could be—hot sun, cool breeze, sailing clouds, and that spring-in-Paris smell of green leaves, flowers everywhere, and sprinkled asphalt.

I was outside, the doors of the school had closed behind me, I was riding in an open horse-drawn carriage across Paris. Then I was sitting in a little noisy train on pearly gray broadcloth—more than slightly spotted. The windows were open, the smell of fields and orchards blew in and also the cinders, one of which immediately got in my eye and was capably removed by Mademoiselle Laroque. Lucie was there and Mademoiselle Lemay and Mademoiselle Pitou and half-a-dozen French girls. And we were to lunch at one of the houses of the order and take part in a procession in honor of the Virgin Mary.

At the village station a black carryall waited, and a frisky little colt ran beside one of the fat horses. The long seats faced each other, and to the smell of horses there was added the smell of new, black, pile cloth from the rolled-up side curtains. We were in a small, sunny village built close to the ground, all of uniform, gray masonry and yellowed plaster, until we saw the flowering treetops above the high walls and smelled the gardens.

The place we went to was walled also, but inside it was like a farm, with a long stone house and stone farm buildings, and there were a number of old people and some children. But what I recall most is the orchard, white with apple blossoms, and beyond, an alley of plane trees under which the long breakfast table was set.

At that time neither foreign influence nor war-raised cost of living had spoiled the superlative French cooking, and that day there was all you wanted to eat of everything. Of that meal I still remember the tiny fresh radishes served with unsweetened butter and the bread, warm and crisp from the oven, the exact taste of the lentil soup followed by a civet of hare [rabbit stew] served with the classic black sauce and the beautiful white hearts of cheese dripping with thick *crème d'isigny* [cream from Isigny]. And there were bowls without end of wild strawberries and apricots. That day we left the table not even able to remember, if we had tried, what it was to be hungry.

I sat beside Mademoiselle Laroque, who was in high spirits, the rich sound of her voice and laughter playing over the long table. She teased me about the Mississippi, asking me if it was indeed larger than the Seine that we could see flowing below at the foot of the sloping pasture.

And when breakfast was eaten we joined the procession of villagers—men, women and children—that wound singing through the streets and out along the lanes between the new green fields, with the priests marching at the head carrying images of the Virgin. Saints taken from their niches rode on platforms, and enormous gold crucifixes shone in the sunlight. Small choirboys and acolytes ran alongside, swinging their censers, chains tinkling, and clouds of incense floated up into the serene sunlit air.

Many of the marchers carried banners and holy images, crosses and garlands of roses. It was the Feast of the Virgin Mary, and many of the young girls of the village wore white dresses. That is the France

I remember, a part of what is France to me. On the way home Mademoiselle Laroque asked me rather scornfully, "Do you have anything like this in your church?"

---

14. A Long, Lonely Summer at School

As summer came I was moved up a flight into a small room under the roof. It was hot there, but there were definite advantages. I could see above the level of the other three wings that enclosed the court. I could breathe up there the air of Paris, smell the overblown foliage, the hot asphalt, the nostalgic scent of warm rain falling on dust. I could see too a panorama of roofs including the steep, slated peak of the old church and also its tower.

The school itself was almost empty. The French girls had gone and most of the foreigners too, except a few of the older ones, among whom was the Polish physiologist who had never spoken to me since the debacle of my musical appearance. I was alone now most of the time. Mademoiselle Pitou and Mademoiselle Martin alternated at our diminished table. Between meals I stayed in my room. Certainly I was not unhappy but existed rather in a state of reverie, turned in completely on myself or lost in the few books I had that I read over and over.

Dickens's *David Copperfield* and Hawthorne's *Wonder Tales* provided, in their opposite ways, worlds of such enchantment that I asked nothing better than to be left in them. At home you were always being dragged away, told to run out and play, to take your nose out of that book, that your eyes would be ruined, and so on.

But now I could turn from the last paragraph of *David Copperfield* back to the first and share again the lives and events I already knew by heart that, unfailingly, made me laugh and cry and shudder in the same delicious way—Murdock, Betsy Trotwood, little Dora, Uriah Heap, Charles Micawber. Or linger undisturbed in Hawthorne's shining world of demigods and heroes. Or float on the smooth cadences of *Philosophe Sous les Toits* [*Philosopher under the Rooftops*], the opening sentence of which still rings pleasantly in my ear. Or, when I was not reading, carry on in my mind an endless rigmarole about two children for whom I invented countless adventures.

At this time too a rather strange thing began to happen. Sometimes just before I wakened in the morning I would see the big face of the clock that hung in our courtyard and the position of the long black hands. The clock was out of line with my room and could only be seen by leaning out of the window. But each time when I hurried to verify what I had dreamed, I would excitedly find the hands in the exact position I had just seen them in my sleep. This brought me a queer kind of happiness. It was as if I was less alone, as if some invisible addition had been made to my life.

And I was accompanied too in another way. Several times during the day—early in the morning, at noon, and again at twilight—the air would be fairly split with the clanging, brazen tumult of church bells. At the first loud note the emptiness about the old tower would suddenly be filled with a chaos of fat pigeons. They would wheel and dart in every direction for a moment, and then, as if all were instantly inspired by one purpose, the whole flock would execute together—and without moving a wing—a long soaring sweep and vanish from my sight. The line of their clean flight would somehow remain as if drawn with a pencil on the sky, and oddly too, I not only saw the line but seemed to hear it, too.

For at that time there began what has sometimes occurred to me since, especially in the Congo forest, where undernourishment also lowered the threshold between senses, so that I seemed to see a sound and hear a color—the drums making a pattern before my eyes, the round red moon a brazen clanging on my ears as it swam up above the forest. And this borrowing by one sense from another enhanced immeasurably the beauty of what was perceived as I learned during that distant summer when almost all I had of the world came through an open attic window.

Once or twice, to be sure, I was taken out. On one occasion Mademoiselle Pitou asked me to walk with her in the green *allées* of the Luxembourg gardens. On another Mademoiselle Martin asked me to go to Robinson for the afternoon. This excursion I definitely did not enjoy. Mademoiselle Martin was large and took up so much room in the bus that I had to sit quite close to her. And at no time, but especially not in summer when she wore the same woolen dress she had worn all winter, was it pleasant to be too close to her.

At Robinson too there was a great deal of noise and dust. I had had no experience of amusement parks, and I could not understand anything about it. I did not know why the little houses were built in the trees, nor was I invited to ride on one of the donkeys, which was the one thing I would have enjoyed. It was a long trip to get there and to get home. Mademoiselle did buy me a *gauffre* [waffle] and a glass of *groseille* [currant] syrup and siphon water, but this was not enough to make me enjoy the occasion.

---

15. The de Vibraye Sisters

Why is it that certain happenings, in themselves of no importance, cause a pain that cannot be forgotten? Happenings that though they may be overlooked for a time nevertheless live on imperishably when so much that one would wish to keep is forever lost?

One by one the demoiselles began to go away to the various houses of the order by the sea or in the mountains. Then the time came when Mademoiselle Laroque was to leave, and the last night before her departure she was to preside at our table. The French girls, as I have said, had left for the summer and were with their families in the country. Their houses in Paris were closed, and if any girl had to spend a night in town, she came to the school.

On this particular summer night it so happened that two of the most charming of them, the sisters Jeanne and Marguerite de Vibraye, were at the school. I had always liked and admired them. They had such pink cheeks, such bright blue eyes and shining teeth, an air of being so exquisitely well cared for. Tonight they wore fresh summer frocks tied around the waist with satin sashes and hair ribbons to match, their feet clad in bronze kid slippers. And in the white twilight the pale colors of their dresses took on the same purity and poignance that flowers take on at dusk.

When I saw them coming across the courtyard to the dining room, I thought that nobody had ever been so beautiful. And suddenly, seeing them like this, I was conscious of my own appearance. Myself.

I was wearing the blue serge sailor suit I had worn all winter, not at all clean and grown too short. My thick hair hung in two long

73

braids fastened at the bottom with elastic as my hair ribbons had worn out. My high black-buttoned shoes were scuffed at toe and heel and their black cloth tops were worn at the ankles. All at once the feeling of the spectacle I must offer almost made me faint. It wasn't possible, I could not sit there at table, a dirty, shabby ragamuffin, beside those two shining creatures. But there I was.

And there was nothing else to be done. If I left now I would be questioned, I would have to come out from behind the chair and table that hid at least half of my unworthy person, brought far more into the public view than I was now. There was nothing else to do but stay and hide as proudly as I could what I felt.

The Paris days are long in June, and it was light as day in the cloister that gave on the pebble-paved court. I knew they would retire there after dinner. Inside the gaslit dining room at least some of my shabbiness had not been seen. But not for anything would I have exposed it to the searching light of that clear white dusk. The moment dinner was over I slipped out of the dining room through the opposite door into a dark hall and ran as fast as I could up the three flights of stairs to my little bedroom under the roof.

It was exactly over the courtyard where they sat in the twilight, and for a long time I heard the easy, happy flow of their voices, the tinkling well-bred voices of the sisters de Vibraye, their laughter, especially the warm, contagious laughter of Mademoiselle Laroque. I loved so to talk, to laugh, to be where people were.

Never before had I felt such mortal sadness. My sadness was so profound and so poignant that it sharpened every sense, stamped every sight and sound for all time, on my memory. The pearl white sky above the courtyard, the stabbing sound of our school bell ringing. I could feel the touch of the counterpane against my girlish body. Never before had I felt so alone, so cut off from all safety and friendship and loving care. And they sat there so long! If they would only go, if the gentle sound of their gay voices, chatting so peacefully in the summer night, would only stop.

At last the chairs scraped, the goodnights were said, and sleep came. And while I slept that secret inner guardian of our early years, whatever it may be, took away my sorrow. And in its place came a dream that I was on the steamer on which we had come to France, that we had stopped in mid-Atlantic at some island. I went ashore there with my family and up the hill to a steep and glittering city, and in the streets stepped friendly unicorns and tall, graceful, smiling gazelles and all the mystical animals that live among the green trees and small, bright, jeweled flowers of a Cluny tapestry.

Then the days grew shorter and cooler, and all the demoiselles and the pupils returned to the school, except for Mademoiselle Laroque, who was in Rome and was not expected until November.

How strongly our senses are persuaded by the seasons. Each one, while it lasts, makes us believe there has never been another. In summer, winter can scarcely be imagined, and in winter, summer is a dream that could not have been real. The midseasons too have their own illusion of eternity, and that year, when autumn came, it immediately seemed as if it had always been like this, with rain slashing at the windows and fog creeping into the cold, airless, gaslit rooms. The school year had begun. Lucie was back and Octavia and the others, and there were new girls too.

————

16. Suzy

I had acquired now another and very different friend. I no longer had to light my own candle or bound across the icy tiles to bring in my own jug of hot water. Suzy did it for me, and it would be waiting beside the bed when I wakened for the few words we exchanged each day. She was a squat creature, sturdy and muscular as a Shetland pony but so extenuated by the life of savage toil she and the other maids lived that her breath came short, her heartbeats shook her strong, small body, and her round black eyes seemed ready to pop out of her face from the pressure of her continuous haste and effort.

"I brought it in for you, Mademoiselle, the jug of water," she would say. "That way you don't have to do it for yourself." Her voice was hoarse and guttural, and she spoke with an indescribably vulgar accent. "And this candle too, it was me lighted it."

"Oh, thank you, Suzy."

"Mais, oui. When one is little, one likes to be spoiled."

How Suzy, of all people, knew that, I cannot imagine. She herself, as I gathered from the fragmentary phrases she blurted out without any preamble but beginning out of some continuous monologue inside herself, had known nothing but appalling hardship. She was, she used to say, repeating, it seemed, a phrase she had heard used about herself, "a child of the gutter." When she was not more than eleven or twelve, she thought, not being certain of her own age, Suzy went into domestic service, and with the exception of a few days off to have a baby at the charity hospital, she had worked ever since.

The baby she had loved a good deal, and the tears would pour down her gross snub-nosed little face when she talked about it.

"It was one of those places in the country," Suzy began one morning, "for the babies of girls that work. I didn't like the place, but what could I do? I had to leave him there." Suddenly, as if she herself were unaware of it, a curtain of tears covered her face. "They buried him before I knew he was sick."

Another day Suzy began: "Maybe I didn't tell you his name? It was Peter Paul. He might as well have two saints as one, I thought. It don't cost any more. And they're the biggest saints there are, Saint Peter and Saint Paul; they're in the first rank. I thought he'd need it, poor little *garçon*."

It was against the rule for maids to come in while the *pensionaires* were in their rooms. So she would risk only a few words. But she never left without asking if there was something she could do for me. "I could steal a bite of food for you, Mademoiselle, when I'm washing the dishes," she would say, or "I could wash out a nightgown for you late at night, after they're all in bed? That way you'd save the price of the laundry." And then, thanking me for I knew not what, she would hurry out, and I'd hear the quick slap-slap of her bast shoes down the stone corridor.

I do not know how it was possible for human beings to work as hard as those women did and live. From early morning until late at night there was the slapping sound of their crude shoes on the stone corridors of the school, half running up and down the endless flights of stairs, carrying jugs of water, emptying slops, answering bells. There were four of them to care for twenty rooms, wait at table, help in the kitchen, clean the shoes. You saw them all over Europe in those remote times and in England too. The *bonnes à tout faire* [housemaids], the slavey of the London boardinghouses, doing backbreaking work for a few dollars a year. Condemned to serve.

At that time I took Suzy for granted, an ignorant chambermaid with a rather stupid face and a way of speaking that was an affront to the ear, who was indeed, before I left, to help me in a difficult time with the most delicate kindness. But why not? Even if I had been older and far wiser I should have thought little of finding this kindness in one of those persons we called servants. It was too usual.

But of late years I have remembered Suzy and others like her—a hunchbacked woman at an inn on the Lake of Zurich, a blue-eyed girl in Geneva, a young woman waitress in the south of France—and the word "servant" has taken on new meaning and stature for me. Has even made me ask myself whether that unremitting work for other people, leaving them no single instant in which to think about themselves, did not elevate at least some of them to saintliness.

———————

17. Growing Up

My own life was complicated now by the fact that I began to have a great deal of pain. I was assailed with backaches so severe that at times I was literally faint with agony. It was a terrible, raging sensation as if strong hands pulled inside me, dragging all the life force out of me.

I spoke of this once to Mademoiselle Martin. Perhaps because she was charged with the *matériel* she seemed the likeliest person to concern herself with daily difficulties. Or perhaps it was merely that she gave me an opening so that it was easier to overcome my shyness.

We were standing at the foot of the staircase. She finished whatever she had been saying to me by adding: "And now, little one, run up as fast as you can or you'll be late for supper."

"But I can't run, Mademoiselle. My back aches so badly I can hardly stand." She stared down at me with her rather stupid pop-eyes. It seemed to me that she reddened slightly. "Ah, but that is merely growth," she said after a moment and turned away.

So it was Suzy who helped me. It was Suzy who of her own accord put hot bricks in the bed when I felt the worst, who came at a certain time with what I needed and which she must have bought with her own money. Nothing was said, not by a single word was the subject directly touched upon.

---

18. More Religious Instruction from Mademoiselle Laroque

After school resumed in the fall Mademoiselle Laroque and I occasionally continued our interviews about religion and the Catholic Church, but each, it became apparent, for different reasons. As we parted after one particular interview—it was more like a lecture—in the grand salon, I heard her saying, " . . . and tell me, my child, did you read the small book I sent you?"

The answer should have been an unqualified yes-and-no, but I'm afraid I said yes. I had glanced at it, but in its different way the booklet had seemed to belong in the category of the Sunday school pamphlets that were perpetually strewn about the house by my grandmother in the hope of correcting the unholy persuasions of a fiercely agnostic father. Puerile tracts relying upon the repetition of weird Palestinian place names, unexplained biblical episodes, and such meaningless phrases as "blood of the lamb."

Mademoiselle Laroque's book had evoked nothing but the grim ugliness of a church basement—the cheap pine furniture, the unshaded light, the hissing of steam, prison bareness not alleviated by paper-chain loops made by even more unfortunate kindergarten pupils, maps of Asia Minor hanging on the plaster walls, the tedious iterations of a young woman without fire or faith, fancy, or imagination. Certainly the natural and poetic religious instincts of childhood must be more thoroughly annihilated by the American Sunday school and everything that emanates from it than by even the disbelief of parents.

In Mademoiselle Laroque's pamphlet the references to a "doux petit Jesu [sweet little Jesus]" left me particularly cold. If a child could conceivably love an abstraction called Jesus, it certainly would not be in the form of a child like himself but at least an adult. But I am sure that for her too, as for me, all this was merely routine and that she was waiting for something else.

As for me, in spite of her boring talk, the spell deepened—the nostalgia for some mystic retreat, some dim gothic heaven illumined only by the divinely burning colors of stained glass and inhabited only by Mademoiselle Laroque and myself.

One cold November day when we were alone in the dining room after lunch she had put her hand, in the old familiar way, on my shoulder and stood smiling in the old way into my face. "But I do believe you have grown taller," she suddenly said. "You have become *une grande jeune fille.*"

We talked for a few moments of nothing in particular, and then she continued. "It worries me to see you, my child, as you are, without faith, without God, without any hope of salvation. Have you thought at all of what we have talked of so much in the past?"

I had to say no. And, too, that I didn't know what to think. She laughed a little and then became grave. "Haven't you felt blind stirrings within you, the signs of spiritual growth and passion, the thirst for true religion . . . ? I shall send you some other books, older books. And next Wednesday, then . . . I will see when I can find time to talk with you."

She got up and we walked together into the vestibule, that entrance to the part of the school the pupils never entered. She had her hand on my shoulder, and as we stood there she slipped it around me, and, drawing me to her, she kissed me on the mouth, not once but many times. Then her gravity gave way to a look of irony that was for herself as well as for us and all the world. "I fear that my petite Grace hasn't the smallest idea of what I'm talking about."

I did not say that I had just felt the same blind stirrings here in the room where we stood. I only said, "Oh, yes, Mademoiselle."

But I think she knew I had. On the one side on which we touched we were as alike as if I had been her child. Though in much else we were so fatefully different that almost the last memory I have of her was her look of proud anger and repudiation. Then, without speaking, she disappeared through the door that went into the private part of the school.

And I, standing where she had left me, knew that something was different. Something in myself. Something that protested, that rose up against her. I knew too that she had kissed me with passion.

In the interval of almost a week that followed Mademoiselle Laroque did not appear at table. Nor did I think of her directly during that time. I did not think of our interviews or of anything she had said or of the way she had kissed me. As always the fact of her existence burned like a light through the neutral haze of school life, but I directed toward it no conscious attention. She had sent me several books, which I had not read, and I did not open them now. Instead I began to read a highly fictionalized version of the *Children's Crusade* that had somehow come into my possession.

Then, suddenly, Mademoiselle Laroque reappeared at our table. As usual, she entered the dining room with an air of haughty gravity and looked at no one until she had asked the blessing. But now, when grace was over and she was sitting down, she swept my face with one swift and terrible look.

"Good God," said Lucie, whom nothing escaped. "What does that mean?"

I did not answer. The thick white plate at my place looked suddenly big with something faintly nauseating about the crisscross lines burned into it by the heat and its smell. There were knife cuts too and a place on the edge that had been chipped. I did not feel hungry. I felt as if I had never seen a plate like this one before and as if I could not eat anything from it.

Lucie had discreetly changed the subject and was chattering softly about something as if nothing had happened, nothing were changed. After a while I began to talk to her too and to Octavia. All at once I said, "I'm going home soon. I've had a letter, and I'm going home at Christmas time."

The violence of sorrow I felt at Mademoiselle Laroque's repudiation had suddenly put its momentum back of this idea of home, made it seem necessary for me to state this, not as a possibility but as a fact. From this moment I believed without question that although that particular day, whatever it was, had not brought the letter announcing my departure, the next day surely would.

To be sure, the scorn or wounded pride or anger or whatever it was that Mademoiselle Laroque's first glance had indicated was not again revealed. Her eyes as they circled the table would pass over or even blankly linger an instant upon me as if I were an inanimate object accidentally found in their orbit. This exile from her pierced my heart, but although I would have been incapable of making any such analysis at the time, it left my pride intact.

I had willed what came about. And yet "willed" in the sense of conscious volition is not the word at all. I had not made a decision; I had obeyed a reflex, made a rejection solely by instinct. We had come to an instinctual parting of the ways. She was or, rather, had been made by life, I am sure, something that I was not.

———————

19. Lily

I had known that Lucie would eventually speak of Mademoiselle Laroque to me, and I felt little interest, only a vague jealousy of the girl in the black veil, the Norwegian pupil we all knew as Lily. It was Lily to whom Mademoiselle Laroque was now giving instruction and who suddenly became the center of a dramatic incident at the school.

"Mademoiselle Laroque," Lucie began explaining to me, "has converted I don't know how many girls, and usually it's quite all right."

"The parents, to be sure, have sometimes made a fuss," she went on, "but they get over it in time. The girl becomes a good Catholic and is saved from going to hell. But this time it is *toute autre chose* [entirely another matter]."

Lily, it seemed, had taken the whole thing too hard. The light of spirituality had dawned for her with embarrassing intensity and glory. Now she was announcing that as soon as she was received into the church she would join the cloistered order of the Carmelite nuns. "Even Mademoiselle Laroque is slightly annoyed at that," Lucie declared.

Lily's father, a Lutheran pastor in Norway, and mother were beside themselves and had sent repeatedly for Lily to come home. She refused, and they had then decided to come to Paris to fetch her. But the mother became quite ill, and the visit had to be postponed. Lily herself had been removed from the foreign section of the school and from her cousin and best friend when she began to receive instruction. The latter, as I had seen, was furious, especially at Mademoiselle Laroque.

"There were such scenes as you couldn't imagine," Lucie exclaimed with relish. The cousin stayed on at the school hoping to influence Lily. At last she saw that was impossible and went back to Norway. And now the parents themselves were about to arrive. Rumor had it that they were bringing a lawyer, that Mademoiselle de Vaugirard had already received the Norwegian consul.

Lucie saw the parents arrive with a French lawyer and a Norwegian lawyer. The wife, she declared, looked exactly as the wife of a Lutheran minister would look on the stage, but the father looked like a prophet fasting in the desert, gaunt and visionary and full of rage.

Now there seemed to be an unusual rush and swish of long skirts along the corridors, and the demoiselles were often seen stopping to speak together in low tones with preoccupied faces. Or at least, stirred by Lucie's excitement, that is what I imagined.

Mademoiselle Laroque, however, continued to preside at our table in rather better form than usual, triumphant, proud, and full of gaiety. And Mademoiselle Pitou, sitting opposite, watched her rather wonderingly, I thought, with a faintly quizzical look in her pinpoint eyes.

Of the goings-on, which lasted several days, Lucie was told a good deal in deepest secrecy by Mademoiselle Lemay, and she promptly passed it on to me. The thing had begun with anger and unpleasant threats. It was within the power of the parents to remove Lily by force, and that was exactly what they proposed to do. One afternoon an archbishop and several priests mounted the silky old stairs and entered the little gothic door behind which Mademoiselle de Vaugirard reigned in her throne room.

Then, all at once, a strange thing happened. The pastor had spent long hours alone with his daughter, and after the last interview he went straight to Mademoiselle de Vaugirard. They would not, he said, interfere any longer. They would say a last good-bye to their daughter and go back to Norway. Which they did. Lucie was on hand to witness the departure and saw them go off, blinded, she said, with tears.

Since then I have wondered if in those long talks together father and daughter did not at some moment pierce beyond the irreconcilable difference of creed into some dimension of pure faith, of mystic revelation, that was possible to them both—and the capacity for which the devout pastor may have known came to her from himself.

In the aftermath all that Lucie managed to learn was that while taking religious instruction from Mademoiselle Laroque, Lily had got herself into a hysterical state over something and that then she was suddenly removed against her will from Mademoiselle Laroque's powerful patronage. Then Lily had made a scene of some kind before her parents. It was not Mademoiselle Laroque's fault, Lucie told me, the girl was unbalanced.

There were other things of which Lucie knew nothing, but the final upshot was that Mademoiselle Laroque left before the second term to enter one of the branch houses in the Pyrénées. She went without bidding me good-bye. That flash of scornful and angry disdain in her proud, dark eyes was the last direct look she ever gave me.

But without her, life at the school lost its color and its strangeness. I spent the long months afterwards in a long childish daydream, that refuge into which a lonely child can so easily and mercifully escape.

---

20. A Disappointment

The winter cold and sleeting rains had begun in earnest, and Christmas no longer existed in a vague future before which anything could happen. It was only ten days distant. My belief, however, that I was to be called for before the holidays and taken back to America did not flag.

And when, early one rainy, blustering afternoon, the door of our classroom opened, and it was announced that a visitor was waiting in the reception room for me, I knew that the confirmation of my faith had come.

I raced across the courtyard and down the gallery and through the swinging doors into the darkly shadowed brightness of the bare room where Mademoiselle Lemay sat behind her desk, stiff-backed and lean, with the unchangeable half-smile fixed on her bony, priestlike face.

In the corner nearest the door I saw the lady who had brought me here more than a year ago. Her black coat and the coarse dark fur about her throat were spangled with moisture, and she was tugging at the small veil she wore fastened under chin. She could not loosen it, so she kissed my cheek briefly through the net.

"Good gracious, child." She was still seated, and, taking hold of me at arm's length, she said, "For goodness sake, what an awful dress!" And her eyes went to my hair, swept over my dress again down to my heavy, much-darned stockings—so lovingly darned by Suzy—and my worn shoes. "And you've grown too," she said after a minute. "You're too thin, but you have grown."

"Are we going back to America right away?"

She looked at me and opened her eyes wide. "What, America? When did you hear last from your parents there?"

"They said somebody would come for me, and I would be going home . . . we would go to Le Havre and get on the boat."

"Listen, Grace, you are a sensible child. You . . . I am quite sure, that if you read the letter again you would see that . . . you would not think that . . . " She began again.

"I'm sure if you read it again you will find . . . of course it should never have been written, never, never . . . " she added, frowning to herself, " . . . you would find that it said someone might call for you."

Rumble, rumble, shaking under your feet, the dark noise, like the wheels and the horses' hooves, unseen, the black horses of Pluto's chariot . . . it was better than this, than the stale bright air, the empty walls, the whistling of the greenish-white gaslights in the dark, the rosy lean face of Mademoiselle Lemay a skull under the eerie greenish light.

"Now, the fact is, you are a sensible child, Grace. This is a nice school. You are happy here in this school, aren't you? There are lots of little girls like yourself, it's a nice school, the teachers are nice . . . The teachers are nice, aren't they?"

What does a child answer when adults ask these questions?

"Now, don't look at me with those big eyes as if you didn't know what a fortunate little girl you are. The fact is, Grace, that your people thought I would be going home this Christmas. But I'm not. I have to go right back to England, and I shan't get away from there until next summer."

She paused, and after a moment in a voice I never heard her use she said, "But let me tell you something. As soon as I get to London I am going to get you some nice things, Grace. I am going to get you a dress and some nice things and send them right back. You believe . . . Could you tell me about your underwear?" she asked suddenly.

I murmured, "Suzy . . . " and then could not go on.

"Very well, I shall ask Suzy."

"No," I cried. "Please. No, don't speak of Suzy to anybody."

"But why not?" Her eyes narrowed.

I couldn't tell her. It was too long, would be too incoherent. It was too much to tell her about the intricacies of the medieval school, about my five pieces of underwear, that it was Suzy who mended them when her long day's work was done . . .

"I'm afraid I shall have to look into this," she said after an interval in which I could find no words. I knew that to beg her again to say nothing about Suzy would only make her the more determined.

"But in any case," she added magnanimously, "I shall myself see to a new outfit for you. You believe that, don't you?" she asked, rising.

I seemed to hear my mother's voice, speaking of her. "She's never cared for anybody, never really liked anybody in all her life, but she does keep her word."

"And now I'm going to find out from somebody just what you've got and what you need," she said. Then she bent over and kissed me without trying this time to undo her veil.

The swinging doors sighed, closing behind me, and I stepped out into the blowing darkness, this time not needing Mademoiselle Pitou to guide me along the dark, circuitous passageways to my room.

I know that Suzy never blamed me. I tried to tell her, and she knew I had not meant to cause what happened. She bade me farewell through tears that covered her snub-nosed, sturdy, pop-eyed face. I wept too, uncontrollably—I had not cried for so long!—and she assured me they didn't like her anyhow. They had always been waiting, she said, for something like this.

And within the next few days a notice appeared in all the corridors of the school, reaffirming the strict rule that the maids were only to enter the rooms when the *pensionaires* were absent.

[Grace Flandrau's "French School" memoir concludes here, but "Child Memories" mentions that she returned to America the following summer, accompanied by her stepmother and sister, "to see my father die."]

William Blair Flandrau

Mexican Memory

Introduction

William Blair Flandrau of St. Paul, Minnesota, bought his large coffee plantation in the state of Veracruz, Mexico, in 1904 as a twenty-nine-year-old bachelor. During visits to his younger brother's ranch from 1904 to 1908, Charles Macomb Flandrau wrote his famous essays about rural Mexico, published by D. Appleton's in 1908 as *Viva Mexico!* Four subsequent editions made the book a classic on pre-revolutionary Mexico.

In 1909 Blair Flandrau married Grace Hodgson, also of St. Paul, and brought her to his ranch, the Santa Margarita, in the remote mountains near Jalapa, but the times were unpropitious for foreign businessmen in Mexico. Within three years the revolution broke out, and at Blair's insistence, for safety's sake Grace fled the ranch, moving first to Jalapa, then to Mexico City, next to New Orleans, and finally back to Minnesota. There she sought refuge at Charles Flandrau's home in St. Paul for several years. During these years in exile from her husband's ranch, Grace began writing professionally. In 1916 Blair left Mexico and moved back to St. Paul permanently.

Grace Flandrau wrote the following in a sketch for Harvard's Class of 1900 after Blair's death in 1938:

> Long after the Mexican revolution made it impossible for most landowners to return to their properties, Blair continued to spend the winters, as usual, at the Santa Margarita. He was devotedly loved by all the Indians and peons who had been in his employ and for that reason had little to fear from the revolutionary leaders or the bandits who masqueraded as such. It is true they carried away with them almost everything of value they could find, but during their visits, they dined very politely at his table, spent the evening sitting round the edge of the sala, their great hats beside them, their belts bulging with firearms, listening respectfully to the phonograph, and spitting gravely on the floor. Caruso was their favorite.

---

1. Wedding and Honeymoon

My husband always declared it was in 1909, but his half-brother, who is supposed to be infallible in the matter of dates, maintained it was in 1910. I myself could find no dates among my cloudy, romantic memories of that period of my early youth. Besides, nobody cared much unless it was my husband. Then, unexpectedly, somebody found the marriage license, and it was proved that my husband, not perhaps unnaturally, was right. 1909 was the year in which we were married and went to Mexico to live.

And it all came about that summer in a few days. And I remember when he asked me to marry him, I didn't even say yes; I only asked when. He had given me his brother's book, written from Blair's large coffee ranch in Mexico, to read—whether as an enticement or a warning I don't know. If anything had been needed—and nothing was—to make up my mind, it would have been this description of the place where I was to live.

So the wedding took place simply and quickly. The event had to be hurried up a little because of the coffee picking, which would soon begin and for which Blair had to be in Mexico.

So my mother hurried back from California, protesting each mile of the way against such a sudden and extremely ill-advised decision. She disapproved intensely. Mexico! It was altogether too sudden. I was too young to marry anybody, she thought, much less a man who lived on a coffee ranch in the isolated depths of the Mexican jungle, two days' ride by horseback over a mountain trail from the nearest railroad! I was young and horribly spoiled, she reminded me, showing no interest in anything but frivolity. I showed no signs of being the kind of person who would "make good" in a rough ranch house in Mexico!

I gave her the book to read, and she was still less impressed with the advisability of what I wanted to do. Blair's mother and brother were equally dubious. My own feeling about the journey and about the life at the end of the journey was one of extravagant and joyful expectancy.

I look back now to see what was happening in the world in that year to establish it more firmly in your minds than by the somewhat negligible fact that it was the year in which I was married. I say "look back" because at that time I had no interest whatever in outside events. I was younger even in mind than in years and took no interest in anything outside my own affairs.

So I searched the other day through some old newspapers of that year, looking for some special information that I did not find. But many of the facts that I did find took their places so suggestively in the essential pattern that has been woven since that I think it is of interest to recall them.

Theodore Roosevelt was president. In that year King Edward of England died and was succeeded by King George V. And my eye also fell upon a note which if unimportant is nevertheless amusing: "Taft and Teddy in warm embrace. Old friends spend two happy hours together at Oyster Bay."

But here is one of those other headlines that, as I read them the other day, seemed like the foreshadowing of the completed picture that will eventually appear upon the film: "King Manuel safely out of Portugal. Portugal declared a republic." Here is another: "Premier of Spain attempts to curb rule of church. Brings Spain face to face with crisis." And another: "Member of young Chinese revolutionary party shoots uncle of Emperor." And this, which was indicative of both the period that was ending and the one that was beginning: "Society women arrested in garment workers' strike in Chicago. As soon as their identity was discovered they were released immediately." The striking garment workers, it did not need to state, were not.

But the material I looked for I did not find. In all the news of that spring, summer, fall of 1909—to be sure, these were papers published in St. Paul, Minnesota, and St. Paul is a long way from Mexico—there was surprisingly no mention of two pieces of Mexican news, at least one of which has had startling consequences and the relative importance of which has curiously shifted during the subsequent years.

There was, however, something about Mexico. About riots there before the American embassy, demonstrations against the fact that on the Texas border a Mexican had been burned alive by a group of Americans—Texans. The Mexican had shot an American woman. It was a squabble about laundry. The Texas gentlemen had found it much more outrageous, of course, that an American woman should be shot by a Mexican than by an American. So they burned him alive. The press was rather tart with the Mexicans because of these subsequent mild demonstrations before the American embassy. The burning, they said, was a private matter and should not be made an international issue.

Well, what I was looking for was, first, some description of the great centenary celebrations being held in Mexico City that September of 1909. That was an international event. Special missions were sent to Mexico from all over the world. The United Sates sent a large delegation. Personal representatives of the still numerous monarchies were dispatched carrying personal messages of congratulations and esteem as well as stars, garters, medals to the octogenarian and, it was almost believed, immortal man who for thirty years had been president of the republic: Gen. Porfirio Diaz.

There were parades, pageants, balls, receptions glittering with gold lace and jewels. There were music and flowers and champagne in abundance and Aztec dramas acted in Aztec costumes that lasted for days. Fifty thousand school children paraded, taking flowers to the churches.

General and Madame Diaz, the president and his wife, drove about the city heralded by trumpets preceded by clattering republican guards, but so close to the crowds that a hand might have reached forth and touched them. General Diaz might at any time have been shot or even stabbed, but no inimical attempt of any kind was made. On the contrary, the crowds cheered lustily.

A fact of no particular significance at the time, but within the next few years, the period in which Blair's and my early married life began, that fact would appear increasingly amazing. Within a few months of our marriage a political upheaval of extraordinary proportions began in Mexico, bringing about the downfall and exile of Diaz and the launching of a revolution that lasted more than twenty years. But I am getting ahead of my story.

At any rate, the wedding itself took place on the twenty-first of August. I didn't want to wear a wedding dress, I've forgotten now just why—perhaps because the wedding was so hurried—and was married in a white tailored suit with a hat of thin black straw with enormous white plumes. Under my suit I wore a blouse with its high, severely boned collar binding my throat, and the brim of my hat was so broad that it had to be fastened to my pompadour with yard-long pins.

I remember the hours spent waiting between trains in the station near the old Auditorium Hotel, where Blair and I sat alone watching a boy leaning over the little fountain, spitting languidly at the turtles in its basin.

I remember New York too, and, in view of the somewhat universal custom of allowing people a certain privacy on their honeymoon, I remember with some surprise the five days we spent at the Manhattan Hotel waiting for the boat to set sail for Mexico.

A telegram received before we left St. Paul advised that a dear old friend, a French woman, Madame G. who had chaperoned me for a year in St. Paul when my mother was in California, would arrive from the Adirondacks to be with us at the hotel. And, as she was not well and was having considerable trouble with her heart, she was subject to spells and her room would have to adjoin mine.

At the Manhattan we found a second telegram from Boston. It was addressed to Blair. "Am stuck here with friends of my wife's. I can't stand them any longer. Wire me that we are needed and must come at once to New York." The message bore the signature of an old friend of Blair's.

Blair wired, and his friend came to New York, accompanied by his wife and child, to be with us. The next morning Blair's handsome brother-in-law and adorable sister came down from Maine. And my own sister and her husband moved over to the Manhattan Hotel from Staten Island so as not to lose too much time away from us going back and forth on the ferry.

We drove in hansom cabs, we went to a delicious lamp store with my sister-in-law to buy lamps for our coffee plantation, we lunched in the green-ferny summer dining room of Sherry's, which, at that time, was still a quiet, elegant, and little-known restaurant.

---

2. Passengers Aboard Ship En Route to Vera Cruz

Mr. Cathorpe was a stout and, in my opinion, quite old man from Boston, Massachusetts. He was bald, red-faced and spectacled, wheezed when he talked, and was even a little humble before the inaccessibility of my youth and happiness—although that seemed natural enough as it seemed to me to be what all old people outside the severe enchantment of my own age group must feel. And what surprised me was that, in spite of how old Mr. Cathrope appeared to be, he seemed jolly and glad to be alive. I do not remember now what business was taking him to Mexico. I think it was an importing affair of which he was one of the heads.

Indeed, the ship was filled with American men going to Mexico in this glorious time for business there. He was a man of several vocations, two of which were poetry and cooking. He read poetry and he wrote it. He was always sitting on deck with a small volume of poetry in hand unless he could get somebody to listen to him, and then he talked about cooking. He talked especially about a small club of gourmets of which he was a member, and it seemed to me strange that people would form a club for the sole purpose of cooking and eating and talking about food. It was an exclusive circle composed entirely of men as, he assured me, the high practitioners of the arts and other mysteries must be. And from the way he talked it seemed to me that the dishes they prepared must belong altogether outside the realm of what I had until then considered food. Super dishes—the alter ego of nutriment.

Mr. Cathorpe was traveling to Mexico with two people we will call "the Jeremys." There is no effort of memory that will bring Mr. Jeremy back into my mind, although as I give up and start to write these words, perversely, there comes before me the picture of a clean, thick hand and a bristly, short-cut, black-and-white mustache, with a bit of dry, thick, bright red lip beneath it. That must be Mr. Jeremy.

But I have no trouble recalling his wife, Adela Grimes. She was Adela Grimes as well as Mrs. Jeremy because she was a writer. And the reason I remember her is because of the amazing growth of hair upon her chin and throat and even on her cheeks. Soft sparse hairs, fine as silk and an inch long or longer, that waved like seaweed under water. And because of these, which impressed me so strongly and unfavorably, the whole of her rises before me in minute detail. Stubby nose, kind, bright, forthright, blue eyes behind nose glasses—a middle-aged, stoutish woman who, because she was middle-aged and so plain and had these hairs, might have been the greatest writer on earth and still would have remained a person merely pitiable and without interest to the eyes I had then.

But she was not the greatest writer on earth. She wrote happy stories—or rather, a happy story—and she wrote it over and over again. She went to Peru and the Argentine and Mexico and used these places as a background for the story she always wrote—and which, it seems, hundreds of other people are still writing for hundreds of popular magazines today. In her stories, of course, there was always the American girl. She was slim and cool-eyed, she was proud and tender, she had a Gibson profile, and she was, of course, an orphan. They almost always are, so that there can always be an aristocratic aunt or a rich or eccentric guardian.

There was always the American man too. He was lean and bronzed, and he was always an engineer. He didn't smile, he grinned. He was cool-eyed too and proud and tender—or proud and excessively tender because dear Adela Grimes was so much in love with him herself.

Their story, of course, is susceptible to infinite variety—the girl may even smoke, drink, have an illicit love affair—if it is proud and tender enough and wrapped up in sufficiently indirect verbiage. And although it must always look dark for the engineer for about 290 pages, when the gunrunners are safely in jail, he can tell her all, and the happy moment so long anticipated by the reader and the author comes at last.

Adela Grimes gave me one of her books, autographed. And I was as laughing and scornful and cocksure as people are at the age I was. But what do I think about it now? Well, certainly people have a right to write and to read and enjoy what they please, haven't they? But what about the softening, indeed, degrading effect such pap may have upon the minds that read it, you ask.

Well, I'm afraid I don't believe the minds of those who read it and also believe in it are susceptible to being in that sense degraded. I believe that a certain perception of reality, a certain instinct for truth in life and the arts, is born in some people and can neither be given to them nor taken from them. Nor do I think that education has much or, indeed, any effect upon that particular thing, that quick, sharp, deep, emotional sense and love of the tragic, living quality of things, words, feelings, and of fate itself. Too many people who are educated, yes, well educated, like the Adela Grimes kind of thing and slicker perhaps (for it comes in all grades of so-called sophistication), like it while too many uneducated people scorn it.

But she was a right and good person herself, Adela Grimes, and if I did not know she was dead I should not have put down the foregoing.

———

3. Havana

It was early morning when we went ashore in Havana. This was not the first tropical seaport I had known, and I have known many since.

And it seems to me that for each of us there must be a certain climate or countryside or a certain kind of town that offers not only the realization of pure delight but the exciting, rapturous promise of it. And I am sure many people must feel that way about tropical cities by the sea.

For they are all, in whatever part of the world, so strangely alike. They have an indescribable aspect in common—the liquid golden quality of the burning heat, the windy coconut palms leaning toward the sea, the chalky white and pale blue and pink sugar-frosting villas tarnished and blistered by the great winds that blow upon them, and the rains and the sun, and the way you look in passing into the faces of little dark-skinned men in white, indeed blue-white in this sunlight, and into the women's dark and indolent and burning, quiet eyes.

And at night the way the cafés are so brilliantly, so insanely bright (is it against the wandering dark, those sad and dark-burdened airs from far across the empty, lonely places of the sea?), so raucous with electric lights, so loud with talk and the incredible brazen blaring of the phonographs, of the screaming of a woman's voice through her nose in Spanish. The scent of the too-sweet flowers stealing from wet gardens behind high iron grilles, and there is always the slow roaring, the velvety, hushed crashing of the waves along the snow-white beach.

But it was early morning with the sun already like fire when we went ashore in Havana, and there was something in the air too of the rosy shadow made by the wide, pink bride-hat I wore, wreathed in lilacs. We walked slowly past the long line of little waiting victorias [four-wheeled, horse-drawn pleasure carriages], looking for the best horses with the prettiest faces and the smoothest flanks.

We didn't, in the end, get these, because of a lean, dark, wrinkled, desperately smiling face, a man with delicate dark hands outspread eagerly, wooingly, his head held so humbly, so desperately sideways as if to say, "I know what I have to offer is no good, my cab is old, my horses little withered sacks of bones, so that I never, never will be chosen." So that we got into his carriage and the leather of the seat was burning hot to touch, two wheels were loose, and the ragged bit of carpet was filled with glass.

But when we set off, the wild, crooked wheeling, the mad cracking of the whip above the skeleton backs of the little horses, whose shambling clatter and effort, advancing us scarcely at all, nevertheless gave the illusion of tempestuous speed, of a wild racing, an ultimate and heroic charge.

This is what I remember about Havana: burning white twilight in the crooked downtown streets under the white awnings stretched across them, shops open like bazaars, the racing, whip-cracking shouting of the hundred equipages like our own, the clang and clatter and screaming brakes of streetcars, the hawkers yelling. All made—though there were few automobiles—a din unequalled by the noise of any other city in the world.

Then out, past the cake-frosting villas, the high-walled gardens, the blowing palms, along the flamboyant curve of the bay augmenting the blue dazzle of the sea itself, sparkling near shore but soon losing its frivolous tinsel in a grave, ineffable blueness, a still rapture of color that spread away and away and away to the ultimate rim, to the never-to-be-reached horizon that takes its gold light from another world.

It was on that evening, while the ship was still anchored at Havana, that I first happened to notice Madame Gonzales. We were all sitting in the bar waiting for the ship to sail when I looked across the room and saw a pretty woman. She had blue eyes, a fine, fair English skin, and a black lace mantilla draped over her ash-blond hair. She caught my glance and smiled, and later, we began to talk. I told her, confidentially, that I had just been married and wondered why she laughed so merrily at this piece of secret information. And next night we met again at Mr. Cathorpe's party.

For Mr. Cathorpe was entertaining at supper. The time indicated was nine o'clock, and, as most of us had risen from the dinner table scarcely an hour before this, the hour was felt to be a mistake. But of course the kitchen, to which Mr. Cathorpe was to be allowed personal access, closed at nine o'clock.

As a matter of fact, the dinner hour was of less importance than it sounds because of the poor quality of food on board the *Mexico.* The Ward Line had a monopoly on water travel to Vera Cruz, and the consequence was that if you were experienced and also wise you brought most of what you expected to eat with you. Especially eggs and butter. It was good to be supplied with fresh fruit, tins of biscuits, and a little cheese.

Still, there were meals of sorts, and you did sit in the dining room, and you did eat something if you could. But it was almost too hot to eat. The gulf was breathlessly calm, sea and sky indivisible, a macrocosm of shining cerulean blue through which winged fish soared and oily dolphins looped and slid. There was not enough breeze to dry the sweat that burned on your skin, and greasy smoke sifted down over everything from the black plume that unfurled too languidly in the wake of the vessel.

It was especially hot in the dining room, so recently emptied of diners and still smelling of crumbs and soup and hot dishwater. Mr.

Cathorpe's table was laid with a clean cloth and was ornamented with a fading bouquet of red camellias bought in Havana and a little forest of American flags. Everybody was glad to see there was to be champagne.

The captain was the guest of honor. He was a small, rubbery man, stiff-backed and upright, with the kind of face that is made of red, pneumatic folds of flesh all of a kind, the lips no different from the face, so that his mouth was merely a large irregular gap with large teeth, several of which were conspicuously missing. And he had the deep-set, twinkling, three-cornered eyes of your true mariner.

He began to talk to me at once about what he called "widdas," repeating the not-altogether-original statement that you never could tell about them. You couldn't tell either, for that matter, about passengers as a whole, and when they were both passengers and "widdas" . . . not that he had known she was one. That was just the point.

She had come aboard dressed to kill in some kind of saucy, red shirtwaist and "was as cute a piece as a man would want to see in a month of Sundays. And she sure played hob with the men, had 'em around like flies 'round a saucer of molasses—officers too. 'Conchita' was her name. Big shiny eyes and one of them little noses.

"Well, ma'am, I forgot to tell you too that we had a stiff aboard. He had been the assistant counsel or whatever from New York City, and he died of heart disease. So the Cuban government was going to send quite a delegation to the ship to meet the body. And by jinks, when we came into port I saw somebody came up on deck I never saw before. Widda dressed up in black crepe that would scare you to look and crying and taking on fit to kill when the silk hats come aboard. 'Who in tarnation is that?' I asked the doctor. 'I never seen her before.'

"'Sure you did, Captain. That's Conchita.'

"'Well, what's the fancy dress for?'

"'Why, don't you know, Captain? She's the wife of the stiff aft.'"

The captain choked, he roared, he wheezed, tears streamed from his eyes, a white crumb appeared mysteriously on his lip. "Wife of the stiff aft," he cried whenever he could speak. It was evidently his favorite tale, and we were grateful for it.

It gave us something to talk about during the eternity of waiting that followed. While the master epicure was in the galley preparing his masterpiece we said everything that could be said about widows and about Cubans. We sweated and fanned ourselves until the camellias turned black and the American flags wilted, and then at last Mr. Cathorpe appeared, followed by the waiters. He was flushed and happy and anxious as a man is after a bout with his genius. And the pièce de résistance turned out to be—incredibly—sardines chopped up in scrambled eggs.

Maybe there was something special about the scrambled eggs, a touch of refinement I was too young to appreciate. The young, of course, are notoriously ignorant of the fine points of epicureanism. I don't know. Maybe they were good, and I didn't know it. Mr. Cathorpe's poetry certainly was not good, and I did know it. But youth is more knowing when it comes to poetry.

Nothing in later years has led me to believe that a bad poet can be a good cook. A good cook, a *really* good cook, is a superior person, a person of distinguished intelligence, of humor, discernment, scrupulousness, and sound taste. Not necessarily a good poet, of course, but certainly never a bad one.

4. Vera Cruz

There must have been good-byes said, calling cards exchanged, addresses noted, but I remember none of that. That the customs officials should kindly consent, for a consideration, not to open the twenty-seven trunks and packing boxes seemed natural enough; it was to be expected that everything should be made easy for us.

I do not particularly remember the people at this place beyond an impression of copper-colored faces, shawled heads, the white pajamas of the Indians, so white in the blazing sun.

What I do remember is the sunbaked, half-finished look of the place, old, new and never-finished, which belongs to all tropic seaports, the noise and dust, heat, the smells of garbage, urine, sewers and flowers, and the sea. The little tables spread under the cool arches of the *portales* [doorways], the sinister, lurching, teetering, slightly maniacal movements of the countless vultures who tumbled and flopped with outstretched beaks and uplifted wings about the refuse in the main square, and how they moved, suave and beautiful, when they left the ground, planing on wide wings above the tepid streets, in all the heavenward beauty of their flight and with all the earthly fury of their fierce telescopic eyes peering for carrion.

And I can still see the huge platter of red snapper with red sauce and golden grease with wilted herbs and peppercorns Mr. Cathorpe devoured. And "they've got us beat on the sauces," I remember as the last of the poet's words I was ever to hear.

Recollected too is our compartment in the narrow-gauge train, gritty with cinders and choking with the gas of soft coal, so tiny that there was room only for me. And I can see the so-American face of the

American conductor saying, "Hey, Bill. Glad to see ya." (Blair's full name was William Blair Flandrau.) And, reproachful, lowering his voice, "What the hell'd you buy a ticket for?" And Blair telling me he had played poker twice with these trainmen in Jalapa, firemen and engineers too, and that the legend was that all these American trainmen worked on Mexican railroads because they'd been caught at something that wouldn't be tolerated in the United States—dishonesty or drunkenness or causing wrecks.

5. Arrival in Jalapa

But safe we traveled with them that night across the flat coastland and then up, up, and up over the high gorges on spider trestles to Jalapa. It was the route of the conquistadors when they accomplished that journey that no telling can make credible, which will remain forever something that could not be done and was, so that in an altogether impossible way this handful of ruffians took Europe into the heart of the Aztec empire.

And over the way they traveled and on which they perished and survived I passed so drowned in sleep that to be shaken awake just before dawn was like coming back from death itself. I was wakened just as the train entered Jalapa, because Blair and the conductor had spent the night reminiscing and drinking beer and had forgotten to call me. And I landed in a nightgown and overcoat, shivering in the pure mountain air that was fragrant with orange blossoms.

A streetcar drawn by ten mules took passengers from the station to the main part of town. The car itself managed to stay on the track, but the wildly galloping mules did not. They dashed into arched doorways to break into green patios, tried to climb stairs, or else turned and whimsically insisted on going back instead of forward with an appalling tangle of harness and reins, with the conductor yelling at the top of his voice while cracking his whip like shots from a pistol. The car rocked over the rails laid over rough cobbles, dawn whitened in the narrow streets, and the odor of tropical foliage became incongruously strong in these dark, cavernous, masonry tunnels. Then, with a wrenching of brakes, all ten mules sat down on their haunches. We had arrived at the Gran Hotel.

To write about a Mexican town nowadays is like painting a picture from a picture already painted. It's like playing a tune everybody knows backwards and by heart. You can't get away from speaking about the color, the sunlight, the flowers, the movement.

And the long mule trains, the arrieros, straight and hard as steel, courtly and upright in their great saddles, with their great hats tied under their chins. And the tiny, laden, suffering donkeys, the white-pajamaed Indians walking beside them, the women with brilliant skirts swishing about their feet, their heads wrapped meek and nunlike in their everlasting rebozos.

You're struck by the poise and long line of a woman's body when she walks with an olla of water on her head from the fountain in the public square or a tin of gasoline, her arm uplifted, her back arched to establish her balance. And the endless soft clatter of little hooves on cobblestones, the shuffle of sandaled feet, the soft voices of the Indians, the shrill, nasal staccato of the Mexicans, the church bells that ring and ring and ring, or did, I should say, at that distant time. Not mandatory but insistent and persuasive, ringing and then waiting, as if for an answer that did not fail to come, ringing and stopping and ringing again, beginning before dawn, ringing at intervals all the livelong day until vespers and dark came and later, if a fiesta were on hand.

And the slow streams that never stopped running, as waters do, seeking their lowest level, pouring endlessly through the churches. Men and women and children, babies and dogs, do go into churches, their home, their theatre, their paradise—possibly, many would say, their darkest enemy. Often in the old cathedrals you would see kneeling one of the mountain Indians with a wild dark face, his great hat pressed to his breast, his gaze drowned in the candlelit, liquid-gold beauty of the altar, so radiant after the incredible destitution of his dark thatched hut.

Across from the Gran Hotel was the public fountain, a round basin, blue-tiled, with fresh running water, and the Favorita Café, from which cocktails called the "Don Frederico"—after the man who brought my husband to Mexico—were made and sent across to the hotel.

And beyond that was the house of the owner of most of the houses in the block. Don Alfredo Marvoli had spent all his life from babyhood in a barred room, crawling about the floor on his hands and knees and making sounds we sometimes heard from our balcony, strange grunts and roars and bestial babbling when his food was brought and thrust in to him. But who, as such people were then in Mexico, was kept at home, or, if the imbecile, the madman, or monster happened to be harmless, roamed the streets and added to the medieval flavor that was so strong in the Mexico of that time.

Yes, but not all Mexican cities are set as Jalapa is, high up in a green valley, lush with sugar and coffee plantations and surrounded on all sides by purple mountains, which, because of the combination of mist and sunlight, have a look of transparency, a cloudlike, Olympian, mountainous beauty other cities do not have. For here it rains all the year 'round, and there's always the smell of coffee, wetness, green things and tropical flowers in bloom. All the verdure and fertility about it made Jalapa the center of the coffee-growing region, and ranchers as far away as we were and others still farther sent their coffee crops in by mule train to the local office of the American coffee-buying firm. Sugar, too, and vanilla and oranges helped make it an important commercial place, and it was also the capital of the state of Veracruz.

But I was impatient to leave, I wanted to go to that place across the mountain that was to be forever my home. The mules and Indians, however, had not yet arrived. But we knew all about how it was out there.

Why would it not be my home forever? Everything was so serene, so settled, everybody had his correct place under the sun. We, the foreigners with capital, were almost in the top of the hierarchy. Only the handful who ruled Mexico at that time were higher. We brought money into the country that was much needed for development. Roads and railroads must be built, tropical products raised; even manufacturing by machine was beginning on a considerable scale.

Money was needed, and it couldn't be got out of the great masses because they didn't have it. They didn't have anything at all. Only their strong bodies and their power to work. Not much good to be got out of the top, I fancy, out of the immensely rich landowners, because they were the oligarchy who ruled and naturally would not be too severe upon themselves.

There was, of course, the middle class—the businessmen, shop owners, small rancheros, and so on—and they, more than anybody, welcomed foreign capital to develop the country and lighten the burden of taxation, which fell almost entirely upon them. It was all so settled, and everybody knew and kept his place under the sun.

So that it was as if all our certainties, the precious certainties of our time and class, reached their greatest confirmation here in this ancient little capital city of the state of Veracruz, the state so wisely ruled by that fine gentleman, Theodoro Dehesa, close friend of the great old dictator himself, Porfirio Diaz.

Dehesa's father, it was said, had once offered asylum on his ship to the dictator, who, during one early revolution, had been obliged to flee to Veracruz for his life, and it was Diaz's custom to reward his friends well.

It was pleasant enough, too, in Jalapa. Blair knew everybody, and everybody liked him—the Indians, the peons, the arrieros, the cargadores, the waiters and bartenders. "Buenos dias, Don Guillermo," a soft voice would speak, and we would turn to see handsome X__ or X__ in his white cargadores suit, his looped rope over his shoulder, half-flattened against the stone front of some building in the shade, waiting for the next job.

These were among the men who, all during the first morning we were in Jalapa, kept arriving at the hotel, one with my enormous wardrobe trunk on his head, another with a packing box weighing hundreds of pounds, having run, not walked, all the uphill mile or more from the station. And these and all the rest spoke humbly and politely, they got off the sidewalk for the foreigners or their own upper classes to pass, they kept their eyes lowered, and they received without a murmur the incredibly low wage for which they sold their strength.

It was pleasant to be in the Gran Hotel, its tiled floors were so scrubbed and clean, its great rooms so high and cool, even if the partitions were only of paper with a canvas ceiling stretched above so that every sound and murmur could be heard, even if there was a fiery old English major who armed himself with a trumpet and blew upon it deafeningly whenever there were sounds he objected to until they ceased.

And it was pleasant too to have known men like Don Alberto Lopez who owned the hotel, people who made speeches and were fond of using the words "honorable gentlemen." And to hear them you would think individuals who could qualify for that designation were above reproach.

---

6. Preparing for the Journey to the Ranch

The journey from Jalapa to Misantla, the small village nearest Blair's ranch, and the preparations for getting there are at all times quite a job. You must notify far in advance by letter the approximate date you expect to arrive in Jalapa so that the mules and saddle horses will come in and meet you there. This is when you are alone or have another man or so who is coming to visit you. But when you have to take anyone you love over the mountains to Misantla, such as your wife, it is more complicated.

In that case you have to go into detail in the letter to your head man. You must tell him how old your wife is and how much she weighs, whether she must be carried all the way on an Indian's back or whether she can ride her own horse. The trip for comparatively young persons takes a day and a half, and only one night must be spent on the road. But when you have your wife, two nights must be spent on the road.

You state in your letter that you want ten Totonac Indians (famous carriers for centuries) with a "capitan," who is in charge of them. Your headman sends a runner to a little Indian town to make these arrangements. The capitan picks out ten of his best men, and on the appointed date they are all in Jalapa waiting for you, together with your own men from the ranch with the horses and mules. These Indians are to carry to the ranch, in addition to your wife if she can't ride a horse, such things as a mattress, an oil-stove heater, a cot, pillows, a camp chair, blankets, and any other things that may come in handy on the trip.

When they arrive in Jalapa all the Indians and your own men go to a "mason," which is a combination of stable and dark, dank rooms for the men. They send out a scout to the hotel to see if you have arrived yet. If you have, the whole crowd is apt to come down to greet you, for this is fun for all of them. After shaking hands with them all and asking the condition of the roads (which you know are terrible before you ask) and how everything is going on the ranch, you give the capitan of the Indians some money to buy drinks for his men and tell them to come around the next morning to pick you up.

We were sitting in the *portales* of the Hotel Mexico on the cathedral square when they arrived. They materialized suddenly and quietly out of the passing throng and stood grave and dignified in the clean blouses and tight-fitted cotton trousers they had taken the trouble to change into after the journey. With them were Sylvestre, who ran a regular mule transport of his own between Jalapa and Misantla, and Luis, the mozo from the ranch.

Sylvestre, tall, broad-shouldered, powerful and upright, had a broad, honest Indian face and sparse, drooping black moustache. A man whom, at all times and through all changes, you could trust. Luis was different. He was fair, with little or no Indian blood, with shifty, small eyes and a bad mouth.

Blair and Sylvestre talked for several moments, but at that time I could not understand. Yet I liked their grave reserve and dignified manner. The journey, it seemed, had been safely accomplished; the road was not too bad. Men, mules, and horses were at the mason, and there were eight San Juan Indians to carry the señora over the bad places.

It looked like a small army when they assembled in the narrow street before the Gran Hotel next day. Blair's favorite and beloved mule, known only as "El Macho," was there and a new, handsome, black mule for me, groomed so that, as Sylvestre murmured, running his hand down her flank, one could see oneself in her sides. And there was a new horsehair bridle in patterns so magnificent, so ornamented with pink and blue and orange tassels and rosettes that it was with a grin of almost embarrassed ecstasy that he drew Blair's attention to it. The sidesaddle for me belonged to Señor Weatherstan (a neighbor of Blair's) and had a safety stirrup and a lovely suede seat.

And the equestrienne for whom all this effort had been made was about to embark on a two-day journey over the most narrow mountain trail that for many, many miles was nothing more than a mud path, with two rivers that must be swum on horseback. She was attired as follows: a black Bonardi riding habit made excessively snug with a tight-fitted jacket ribbed with actual whale bones, a McLaughlin riding shirt with high, starched white stock, a hard felt sailor hat for riding, polished black riding boots never made to touch anything but a stirrup, and of course the flowing sidesaddle skirt. Underneath this appropriate getup was a steel, armor-plate corset known in the popular song as the "straight front XYZ."

Well, you only make your debut as a bride in a new countryside once, and I suppose such sartorial effort was only natural for someone on her honeymoon. Well, I was a bride and young; I suppose I didn't want any old Jalapeña to suggest that I didn't know what was what.

Two ladies—Maria, the cook, and Maria, the housemaid, newly engaged—had joined the caravan. They look, in my memory, strangely alike. The same small, oval lacquered heads, shining black hair parted straight down the middle and hanging in two braids. Dark faces with almond-shaped eyes, black, humorous, meek and sly, kind and female, tiny in stature with fine little hands and feet, great bulbous breasts that hung pear-shaped inside their clean cotton dresses, with blouses of red and pink organdy, respectively, trimmed with bright blue and bright yellow laces. Their riding skirts were ruffled and full and made with trains, and they were each hoisted onto small horses into men's saddles on which, with scrupulous modesty, they sat sideways. With wide-brimmed, men's straw hats tied firmly under their chins, they were a strange picture.

"Can she cook?" I asked Blair.

"Can you cook?" he asked Maria.

"Well, señor, to tell the pure truth, not much. But I can play the guitar."

And, indeed, the guitar was with us, strapped on a pack mule along with all the rest of their personal effects tied in two enormous bundles wrapped in calico.

I remember my wardrobe trunk and Luis cursing and yanking at the girths with all his might, his delicate spurred boot pressed against the mule's side, and the great horn of the phonograph peering out of another load, and all the other boxes and small pieces of luggage and the spirit lamp. There were thirty or forty animals in all, and there was an endless clatter and yelling, swearing, and balking before the loads were roped securely to the packsaddles and nicely balanced one side against the other.

Meanwhile, in a silent group by themselves, were the San Juan Indians. It seems to me when I write of these men, and such of their women as I knew, I should have some other medium than words. It should be crayons or pigment with a brush, or it should be a certain arrangement of sounds laid one upon the other, suggestive of ancient places, of something human and nonhuman, as primordial as the thick, dark clamor of frogs, the clear whistle too of a bird or an animal that lives in high, cold places. There should be a beat of sacrificial drums and the soft, pulsing sound of bare feet tracking forest paths. The sound of flint hammers on rocks, of prayers stranger than any prayers we know, and other voices of men and women singing to the goddess mother: Corn, goddess of life.

They stand apart, patient, their faces dark, their eyes immense, smudged with black lashes, long and queer-shaped like Egyptian eyes. Their wild black hair comes down in long bangs over those black and unknown eyes, gleaming with a strange docility and fear.

For who can conceive of the helplessness of this people? Not only could they not read or write, but they do not even speak the language of this land where they live. The language, that is, of the usurpers. They spoke only Totonac, as yet an unwritten tongue, I believe, and they know nothing. They didn't know, for instance, Blair said, that Porfirio Diaz is president of Mexico. They don't know that Mexico has a president or what a president is. They live up among the rocks in their high villages, planting and reaping their corn. That's all they know.

These San Juan Indians are short in stature, and the strength of their muscles is beyond our knowing altogether. They can run for days carrying great loads, no one knows how much. Their powerful shoulders and legs are hidden under the loose white pajamas they wear. Their broad, bare feet, with each toe separate from the others, are planted firmly on the ground and soled with a piece of leather held in place by a thong passing between the great toe and wound about the ankle. And they stand bent a little forward because there is a broad strap around their foreheads, and to this, resting sideways on their shoulders, is fastened a basket, ingeniously woven of reeds and vines, a bed with cushions Luis has thought to bring from the ranch.

The loads are all strapped, it is time to mount. We leave the balcony and go downstairs, but before us we see a luncheon given by His Excellency, the governor of Veracruz. His Excellency, who is also just leaving the hotel, is wearing a white silk hat, white spats, a flawless cutaway, a virginal white piqué waistcoat of the most sublime purity and elegance. And as he steps out of the doorway, El Macho, who has been expecting Blair, rushes forward, past the two soldiers standing at attention, across the sidewalk and thrusts his long mule muzzle, splotched with green foam, against the snowy vest.

But the governor is a sportsman and a lover of animals. What is a waistcoat more or less to him? And when you feel yourself so secure, so powerful, you're not so touchy about your dignity. He laughs, the guests laugh too, the soldiers put back their bayonets, the party passes down the street, and Blair gives El Macho the sugar he was looking for, before we mount.

――――――――

[The continuation of Grace Flandrau's Mexican memoir lies in her handwritten "Mexican diaries" in her papers in Tucson.]

References

Preface

1. The Flandrau Family Papers (hereafter FFP), MS 1018, constitute a 9,000-document collection in the custody of the Arizona Historical Society in Tucson. The papers include those of Charles E. Flandrau (Minnesota pioneer, Indian agent, jurist, and lawyer), his wife, Rebecca Blair McClure Riddle Flandrau, his four children—Martha Flandrau Selmes, Sally Flandrau Cutcheon, Charles Macomb Flandrau, and William Blair Flandrau—and his stepson, John Wallace Riddle.

   The collection also includes Grace Flandrau's papers—the largest segment—as well as those of her father, Edward John Hodgson. Copies of a number of the C. E. Flandrau and C. M. Flandrau papers reside in the Minnesota Historical Society (hereafter MHS) collections in St. Paul.

   Grace H. Flandrau decided to leave the FFP to her husband's great-nephew, the late John S. (Jack) Greenway, great-grandson of Charles Eugene Flandrau, but she deposited them for safekeeping in 1962 in a vault at the MHS pending final disposition. Grace Flandrau left a bequest of $100,000 to the society to "keep the Flandrau name alive in Minnesota history."

   After Grace Flandrau's death in 1971, Jack Greenway, an attorney whose parents were prominent in Arizona history and whose family owned the Arizona Inn, brought the FFP to Tucson and stored them in their original cartons on his back porch at the inn. In 1979, after familiarizing himself with the papers, Greenway returned them to the MHS, where they were placed in new cartons and again stored in a vault, pending his final decision on disposition. In 1984, Greenway decided to bring the papers back to Tucson, where he placed them in the permanent custody of the Arizona Historical Society and participated in cataloging them.

Upon Greenway's death in 1995, his niece, Patty Ferguson Doar, and his stepsister, Saranne King Newman, inherited the FFP. Both are Tucson residents who knew the elderly Grace Flandrau well.

2. Grace Flandrau's papers at the Arizona Historical Society hold a few originals of Maxwell E. Perkins's letters to her, as well as copies of her letters to him, but many of Perkins's original letters to her are missing from that collection. Carbon copies of all of Perkins's letters to Flandrau, however, as well as originals of all her letters to him, reside in the Charles Scribner's Sons Archive at the Firestone Library, Princeton, N.J. The bulk of their correspondence took place between 1930 and 1937.

3. John S. Greenway granted permission, in writing, to Georgia (DeCoster) Ray, to quote from and publish Grace Flandrau's memoirs, *Child Memories*, on December 19, 1991.

Introduction

1. Georgia Ray's forthcoming biography of Grace Flandrau will reveal details of her life and literary career.

2. Charles Macomb Flandrau to Martha Flandrau Selmes, Sept. 1910 and Feb. 23, May 17, and June 7, 1921, Flandrau Letters (copies of originals in FFP), MHS; Lawrence Peter Haeg, "Little Corners of Great Places: The Private Life of Charles Macomb Flandrau," MHS, 278; Charles M. Flandrau to Grace Flandrau, June 8, 1925, file 7, box 2, FFP; D. P. Scrief, "Viva Flandrau," *Twin Cities* (Feb. 1986): 31.

3. Grace Flandrau to Kyle S. Crichton, [winter 1934?], file 30, box 14, FFP.

4. Anna R. Hodson's death certificate, Hennepin County records; Blair Flandrau to Grace Flandrau, May 8 and June 6, 1932, file 27, box 59, FFP; William Hodson obituary, *Minneapolis Tribune*, Jan. 21, 1943.

5. *History of the Hamline University When Located at Red Wing . . . from 1854–1869* (St. Paul Alumni Association, 1907), 172; Grace Flandrau to Theodate Pope Riddle, [late summer, 1930?], Isle of Man, Hill-Stead Museum Archive, Farmington, Conn.
6. Corrin H. Hodgson (great-nephew of Edward J. Hodgson), telephone interview by Georgia Ray, Dec. 12, 1992.
7. William Hodson obituary; Blair Flandrau to Grace Flandrau, May 8 and June 6, 1932, file 27, box 59, FFP.
8. Brenda Ueland, "Among Those We Know," *Golfer and Sportsman* 15 (Dec. 1934): 26; Kate Skiles Klein, conversation with Georgia Ray, June 23, 1993; Grace Flandrau, *New York Tribune*, Feb. 23, 1923.
9. See Maxwell E. Perkins's letters to Grace Flandrau, June 6, 1930, Jan. 25, 1933, Apr. 19, 1935, July 17, 1935, Oct. 13, 1936, and Nov. 8, 1937, file I, box 50, Scribner's Archive.
10. Grace Flandrau to Perkins, June 25, 1935, and Perkins to Grace Flandrau, July 17, 1935, file I, box 50, Scribner's Archive.
11. Grace Flandrau to Perkins, [October or November, 1936?], file II, box 50, Scribner's Archive.
12. Perkins to Grace Flandrau, Oct. 13, 1936, file II, box 50, Scribner's Archive.
13. Grace Flandrau to Perkins, [late 1936 or early 1937], file II, box 50, Scribner's Archive.
14. Although Perkins consistently advised Grace Flandrau to produce a new novel before she published more short fiction, he and Charles Scribner finally yielded to her wishes and published *Under the Sun*, a collection of her short stories on Africa, in October 1936. The book received good reviews but failed commercially. Grace Flandrau to Perkins, [Nov. 1936?], file II, box 50, Scribner's Archive.
15. Perkins to Grace Flandrau, Nov. 2, 1936, file II, box 50, Scribner's Archive; Grace Flandrau, Notes and Diaries, file 471, box 50, FFP.

About Grace Flandrau

Grace Flandrau achieved international recognition from 1912 to 1955 as a writer of short fiction, novels, and nonfiction. The St. Paul author's first stories and sketches of light social satire, cleverness, and sophistication appeared in *Sunset, McClure's, Saturday Evening Post, Ainslee's, The Smart Set, Harper's Monthly,* and *Hearst's International* from 1912 to 1923.

After World War I she wrote novels in the Mannerist genre. The first two, *Cousin Julia* in 1917 and *Being Respectable* in 1923, became Hollywood films. A British edition of *Being Respectable* appeared in 1924, and Scott Fitzgerald told Grace that Edith Wharton called it the best American novel she had come upon in years.

When Lost Generation voices championed realism, Flandrau turned to journalism, and the Great Northern Railway hired her from 1924 to 1927 to write eleven pamphlets on the opening of the Western frontier. Her first modern book—*Then I Saw the Congo,* describing her six-month journey across Africa with friends—received international praise. A British edition of the book appeared in 1930.

Scribner's magazine published twelve of Grace Flandrau's short stories from 1930 to 1936. Maxwell Perkins, Charles Scribner's Sons' executive editor, rated "One Way of Love," her 1930 story, "magnificent." Upon reading "The Happiest Time" in 1932, *Scribner's* associate editor Kyle S. Crichton said she belonged "with the very first of American writers." Author/editor Kay Boyle included nine of Flandrau's sketches in her *365 Days* in 1936. Flandrau became a sought-after public speaker, hosted a show on KSTP Radio, and wrote a weekly column for the *St. Paul Dispatch.*

Grace Flandrau's last short fiction appeared in the *New Yorker, Collier's, Harper's, McCall's,* and *Good Housekeeping* in the 1940s. *Holiday* published her final nostalgic piece, "Minnesota," in 1955. Nine anthologies include her stories. She died in Connecticut in 1971.

About Georgia Ray

Georgia Ray, a Minnesota writer of local history and biography, has worked for more than a decade to revive the once-famous-but-now-forgotten St. Paul author Grace Hodgson Flandrau. Ray has published two articles on Flandrau—"Saving Grace" (*Mpls St Paul*, February 1998) and "In Search of the Real Grace Flandrau" (*Minnesota History*, Summer 1999) and has recently completed a forthcoming literary biography of Flandrau. The latter story details Flandrau's forty-year career (1912–1955) as an internationally published writer, public speaker, and member of St. Paul society.

Georgia Ray lives with her husband, Albert W. Lindeke Jr., at Sunfish Lake, a suburb of St. Paul.